Arise and Shine

Your Journey of Self-Discovery

Nancy L. Parker

BALBOA.
PRESS
A DIVISION OF HAY HOUSE

Balboa Press books may be ordered through booksellers or by contacting:

Balboa Press
A Division of Hay House
1663 Liberty Drive
Bloomington, IN 47403
www.balboapress.com.au
1 (877) 407-4847

Because of the dynamic nature of the Internet, any web addresses or links contained in this book may have changed since publication and may no longer be valid. The views expressed in this work are solely those of the author and do not necessarily reflect the views of the publisher, and the publisher hereby disclaims any responsibility for them.

The author of this book does not dispense medical advice or prescribe the use of any technique as a form of treatment for physical, emotional, or medical problems without the advice of a physician, either directly or indirectly. The intent of the author is only to offer information of a general nature to help you in your quest for emotional and spiritual well-being. In the event you use any of the information in this book for yourself, which is your constitutional right, the author and the publisher assume no responsibility for your actions.

Print information available on the last page.

ISBN: 978-1-5043-1243-1 (sc)
ISBN: 978-1-5043-1244-8 (e)

Balboa Press rev. date: 03/22/2018

CONTENTS

DEDICATION

This book is dedicated to all those who, with courage and faith are leaving the old energy behind; who are turning towards the Light and spreading peace, love and harmony throughout their lives, their families, friends and communitics.

You are truly blessed.

The peace which passes all understanding
Is with us today and always.
The love enshrined within the heart of the universe
Is ours today, and always.

ACKNOWLEDGEMENTS

I would like to acknowledge the love and support I receive from the many Shell Essence Customers/friends who contact me, read my books, and whose warm and positive responses give me confidence to continue writing.

I am very grateful for the ever-ongoing computer work formatting and correcting done by my partner Ken, without whose wonderful help my writing would probably remain as scribbled words in my series of journals.

I would also like to sincerely thank my lovely talented friend Leisle, of small time TV, a Digital Media Content Creative for her many hours of work creating the book covers and author photograph. Leisle also posts my weekly Blogs from this book on FaceBook and the Shell Essence Website and also posts the beautiful artwork.

I'm so very grateful to Renie who helped edit this book, and whose advice and support have been invaluable. Thank you so much Renie.

I'd also like to acknowledge my wonderful Shell Essence staff; Fiona, Michelle, and Marilla who keep my business running efficiently thus allowing me time to write.

PREFACE

In my current life I am the Creator and Owner of Shell Essences – vibrational essences which contain healing frequencies found within the calcium carbonate bodies of specific sea shells, and other crystalline structures. My first book *"Messages from Shells"* describes my journey with shells as well as the stories of those who have taken the essences.

This is my third book, yet I never thought or imagined I would be writing two channelled books using *automatic writing*.

During a short meditation at a Mind Body Spirit Festival, I received a vision of a Being I called *Jesus, my dearest friend*. He drew me through a tunnel of light into a space where together we floated as He gave instructions for a new Shell Essence to be made from the Love with which the universe is created.

Days later, as I was sitting in bed quite perplexed by this unusual experience and wondering what it meant, I heard a voice say *"today and for many days to come, pick up your pen and I will dictate."*

Each morning I sit in bed, and begin with a written request to *Jesus* asking if there is something I could write which would help people today. Even though I think there is nothing more I could possibly write - the words arrive as soon as I put pen to paper.

The *Jesus* who seems to dictate these words is not the *Lord Jesus Christ* I learned about in Christian college, but a person I appeared to know in another life. My automatic writing suggested I was a young lad in that life who knelt in the dust listening to the teachings of *Jesus* and writing them on a manuscript as he spoke. We then hid the manuscripts in a safe house; however a Pharisee in the group discovered where the manuscripts were hidden and destroyed them. Apparently I have been trying for many lifetimes to rewrite them. Until now there hasn't been a safe time.

I have received wonderful feedback regarding that book *Following the Light* I feel very blessed that those words and concepts have helped so many people.

Was this really a past-life experience of the being I call *me*, or have I accessed this story from the *One Mind* to which we are all connected? I have no idea. Does it really matter? No, what is important is the beauty of the material that is being dictated.

I began my working life as an Occupational Therapist many years ago when this therapy first came to Australia. Then, after a friend suggested I was in a *rut!* I spent an interesting couple of years as a Flight Hostess with Qantas Airways in their early days. I started a Natural Therapy practice after completing a few workshops with lovely Denise Linn.

Looking back at my life it seems a bit like automatic writing – no difficult decisions, just a spontaneous flow that still continues.

CHAPTER 1

BEGINNING OUR JOURNEY

Know that each day as you step out of bed,
A new day is dawning, new paths you can tread.
Lessons are waiting; let these not be a chore.
With contentment and love you can open the door.
Bless each word and thought with a positive view
Then clouds can disperse and the sky will be blue.
Create your new day with the greatest of pleasure;
Remember to leave enough time for some leisure.
With a smile and kind words greet each person you meet;
Spread the blessings of peace as you walk down the street.
Now as the sun sets and the birds have retired.
Know you've created the day you desired.
It's time now to take your well-deserved rest,
Feel relaxed and at peace; you are truly blessed.

Whenever you feel sad, confused, or don't know which way to turn, remember you have been here before. You know the way back to fullness and love. You just need to remember it and trust.

From the love within your heart, there is a way back to harmony, compassion, happiness, inner peace and wisdom.

The way you are following isn't always obvious to you or to others; however it's there, taking shape as you start your journey. Please allow this knowledge to resonate within your heart and you will know it's true.

There is so much help available for you now. Please don't let memories of previous difficulties arise to darken your vision. Take the hands of Spirit that are held out to guide you. When the time is right, you will guide others.

This is the first step of your journey. You have had many experiences of repeating old patterns. Now is the time to change direction. The biggest hurdle you will face is your own distrust and anxiety from times now past.

Keep your vision only on your own footsteps – not on what your media is showing you, or where others might choose to go.

This book is written to help you remember. It stimulates an energy flow that connects to your heart, therefore releasing your own heart-centered wisdom.

The Promised Land

We are journeying through the *Promised Land* – that is our Planet Earth. It's called the *Promised Land* because we've promised to create a land of harmony and peace, however despite what we are often seeing at present, this is what we are creating.

Yes, it may appear gloomy and dismal when you look only at media reports, but move your vision closer to home; there are many acts of kindness to be seen and noticed if you look for them. Surprising as it may seem, these small acts are transforming our planet.

Wars, cruelty and barbaric activity have been the noticeable part of our planetary life for centuries. If there had been world-wide media in those days, what would it have been reporting? Now they often must search for isolated acts of aggression and terrorism to make dramatic news.

It's so important to have our vision and hearing tuned toward love and compassion. Search for those small acts and create acts of love and kindness in your everyday life.

Our life-path will then be a journey through *fields of plenty*; beautiful flowers will colour our paths, trees will always shelter us from rain, while storm clouds part and disappear as we approach.

Would you prefer your journey to be through *fields of plenty*, or through streets of warring terrorists? If you look for the flowers, the trees, the fields of plenty, then this is what will surround you. As you expect this peace and beauty, you are creating it, not just for yourself; this path of creation will be followed by many others.

Perhaps some people are hesitant to believe in peace and harmony when they have been taught to look for warring terrorists. They believe they must stay behind strong walls and enclosures to ensure their safety. They see you walking safely in beauty, in peace and may then begin to follow you. As more paths are being created through the fields of plenty, the more peaceful, loving and beautiful our planet will become.

It is always our choice to journey through the *Promised Land*, and those who see the bigger picture, can see a changing landscape. Slowly but surely global warming and acts of aggression are changing to global peace and harmony. This is being created by our intent and an unshakable faith in ourselves and our abilities.

Will you now reset your channels and see beautiful beings creating and journeying through the *Promised Land*?

My life continues to grow with ease and grace
Day by day I create a more loving place

Packing Our Backpack

When you begin any journey you will usually pack a backpack to take with you.

What have you packed in your backpack for this life-journey of discovery - perhaps the most important journey you have ever made?

What we must first pack is our intent; our intended destination. Without intent we might just wander around in circles. What is your intent for your life journey? What do you intend to accomplish? Have you given thought to this? Why have you arrived on Planet Earth at this time? Why are you with this particular family? What gifts might you have carried with you?

Do you carry a map? Perhaps a teaching that is meaningful to you, a spiritual book, or maybe a course in meditation? There are many maps available for life - journeys. So now you have packed your intent and your map. What else will you need to carry with you in your backpack? Will you need some international currency?

International currency is a smile. No matter whom we meet on our journey and what languages they may speak – the language of joy or sadness, hope or hopelessness and courage or fear, a smile of kindness and compassion is understood and felt by every person on our planet.

I was employed as a Qantas Hostess in the early years of that airline, and I remember one day as I was farewelling passengers, an elderly man handed me a note as he disembarked. The note was addressed to *The Hostess with the lovely smile. He wished me joy and happiness in my life, and hoped that no sadness would ever cloud my lovely smile.* I was so touched; I have kept that note among my souvenirs.

No matter what difficulties we may encounter, or how many difficult people we meet who may try to distract us, a non-judgmental smile of kindness will be accepted by all. This is our international currency that will help us through many difficult situations.

Do not rely on the communication of words, as the language of words will not always be understood, and there may be preconceived incorrect notions of what you might be trying to express. Always carry the international currency of smiles.

I also remember a day when I was walking my dogs along an esplanade beside a beach and feeling very sad and despondent. A young man walked past me, looked into my eyes, smiled and said *"Have a nice day"*, then walked on. To my surprise my sadness lifted immediately. I then decided I would always smile and acknowledge each person I passed, and this I've continued to do.

The adornment I wear is always a smile
A happy demeanor is my preferred style.

Achieving Our Goals

When we think about creating and achieving our goals, the first question we need to ask is *What are my goals*? Is it to access more spiritual knowledge? Is it to create better health? A better job? More abundance?

Why do you think you have arrived on this planet at this time? What might you have been hoping to create, and what lessons were you hoping to learn? Will you know when you have achieved your goals, or arrived at your planned destination?

If we have no goals but are just travelling through life from day to day, we may find that we are travelling around and around in circles, retracing our steps from year to year and from lifetime to lifetime. Your life journey is your own personal journey, and I would like you to take out your journal and write your goals; those you intend to achieve on this journey, knowing that they will change. As you master them, new ones will need to be written.

Our intent is already inscribed within our heart, so to access this we will need to meditate, to connect to our heart energy and ask for information; then we can set our goals.

Please do not become despondent if it appears your goals are not being achieved. The time frame you have chosen may not be adequate for everything to fall into place. However if you keep saying your affirmations with trust and faith, and if the goals you have set are in your highest interest and for the highest good of all, then they will manifest as long as your intent continues to be strong.

Do not allow the self-doubt of others to deter you; we have so much more personal power than we currently believe is possible. Perhaps our first goal could be to open our awareness to our powerful abilities that have been denied for centuries, and allow these to manifest without doubt or fear.

As you continue with your life-journey you may find your goals become clearer, or maybe change. As long as you keep your goals in mind, then you will begin to create them, to live them, and to receive the benefits these goals will ultimately bestow on all.

The First Day of the Rest of Our Life

Each day is the first day of the rest of your life. How do you choose to spend it? What will you invest in and what will you gain?

If you consider each day to be one of creativity, what might you require to create your day?

Perhaps you could dispel the feeling of despondency and replace it with a positive feeling? Open your backpack and see what it might contain that you could spend on purchasing the qualities you desire today. Does it contain the gift of more creativity? Whether material, emotional or mind-centered? Great! That's a good start. Does it also contain some special time to spend on that creativity?

Now dig deeper into that backpack; there is something very subtle hidden at the bottom. You draw it out; there is nothing you can see, however there is something you can feel. As you calm your mind you will feel a sense of lovely stillness and peacefulness flowing gently through and around you, something that always lay there waiting for you to uncover and use to create your day.

As you draw out this stillness and peacefulness and wrap it around yourself, your day takes on a very different feeling. You breathe slowly and deeply; any faint feelings of despondency disappear. The question *what should I create today?* now seems irrelevant; you realise that second by second we are always creating. Now the stillness and peacefulness envelopes you; the creativity is flowing naturally and beautifully. You no longer think *I should do this* or *I must do that*. It just seems to happen with no stress or effort.

Synchronicities are a natural part of our day, and we thank and bless them. We now understand that creativity is wisdom, harmony, peacefulness. We have always carried this creativity with us.

No matter what confronting ego demands may cause stress, you can always feel into your bag and take out that wrap of stillness and peacefulness. When you allow these beautiful qualities to flow around and through you, the rest of your life will unfold with the same peace and grace.

Synchronicities are my guiding signs
They show me where the Light of God shines.

Following the Stars

We are arriving at the part of our journey where we are beginning to see that anything is possible. Do not allow self-doubt and hesitation to redirect you. If in doubt, watch for the *stars*, these are signs we can follow.

Just as the mariners of old navigated their voyages of discovery by the stars, so we can also direct our journey by *stars*. These *stars* are little pieces of *light* not necessarily seen by our human eyes but felt by our heart, which is our *steering wheel*.

These *stars* will be synchronicities of acknowledgement and reassurance. When we become aware of them there will be an immediate *oh yes*! a little surge of joyous energy. It may only last an instant, so hold onto it; don't allow its memory to become entangled with doubt and distrust.

No one can create our path for us. There would be no lessons learnt, no triumphs. We are creating our path as we set out on our journey towards the Light, following our inner wisdom. However whenever you feel as if your direction is lost, look into the darkness of your night and watch for the *star* which will be dropped into it. Do not form any expectations regarding how the *star* will appear or you may miss it. Just know that if our intent is to create love, compassion and peace, no matter how dark our night sky may appear, there will always be a *star* of reassurance and love.

Remember the *stars* may come from any direction, yet they are always placed where we will see or hear them, and our heart, our inner wisdom, will respond instantly. If you have missed it, just wait, and when you are ready another *star* will appear. Like the mariners of old, we are setting out on a voyage of discovery with faith and trust that there will be a way. And so there is; watch for the *stars* to guide you.

Recently I was feeling rather blocked and despondent, and wondered if I had been sent a *star* which I had missed. Then I remembered noticing small pieces of chewed paper on the floor beneath one of my bookcases for two consecutive nights. I decided to investigate, and discovered that rats had apparently chewed the back of one of my books, but only one book and the same book each night.

That book was 'The Secret' by Rhonda Byrne, a book I'd bought many years ago. I decided to read it again. To my amazement and delight its message was exactly what I needed to hear; it meant so much more than previously.

Do you know which word will appear when you spell *rats* backwards?

I resonate with beauty and peace
My life flows smoothly without a crease.

Creating Our Spiritual Journey

Our life journey is actually a spiritual journey – a gathering of spiritual wisdom. This doesn't necessarily come from reading spiritual literature, although within every text we may find a prompt to uncover and rediscover our intrinsic spiritual knowledge.

By *spiritual* I mean that which we really are; not a 3D human identifying with an ego personality, but an *energy being,* a multidimensional or quantum being – we do not have words yet to describe that which we actually are.

So little by little, with the help of Planet Earth and all of nature, we are learning to rediscover ourselves. There are many lessons, as we realise what resonates with our heart, our inner being, and what does not. This resonance will keep changing as we experience new adventures. We will leave many old, previously comfortable habits behind. Planet Earth has been seeded with countless opportunities for our growth.

At present we may find ourselves trapped in a very material existence. It could take us a long journey to discover that the spiritual growth we are unconsciously seeking is not found within the material world we are creating. However every small growth and moment of sudden *Aha!* understanding will help us to see the beauty behind the façade of material 3D existence. When we begin to see the hints of beauty and oneness we can start to create this.

At first we will experience and create within the basic dimension in which we feel comfortable, but gradually we will begin to use other non-3D energies. Initially we may find we are continuing to create our life within the context of old negative patterns of greed, competition and competitiveness. But as our wisdom increases, and our resonance with beauty becomes stronger, more familiar and comfortable, we will automatically choose life paths which encourage this growth of love and oneness.

One day the old negative, basic, and slow energy we found so comfortable will seem strange and very unfamiliar. We will move forward on our spiritual journey with more peace and joy than we could previously have imagined.

Love, wisdom and grace
Will always lead us to a better place;
A place that's opening in our heart.
Enter, and a great new life will start.

CHAPTER 2

RE-WRITING OUR BOOK OF LIFE

When we try to re-join our previous path,
The instructions we followed might now make us laugh!
They are being re-written, new directions we need,
That old Book of Life we can no longer read.
Now a new one we're writing, it's held in our heart,
With more love and less fighting, at least that's a start!
So now that we follow a great new direction,
That previous map will need lots of correction.
Let's follow a path with more love and light,
And begin each day with joy and delight.

As we continue our journey through life we may find many things that we had always accepted as *the way things are* will be starting to change. Our 3D life was laid out with well known possible destinations and so-called adventures. It's as if there was a *Book of Human Life* and there was only one volume. We had become familiar with each chapter, and felt very comfortable with the expected beginnings and outcomes.

Now many of those well-read chapters are changing. The words we once knew *off by heart* are fading and disappearing; instead there is a blank page. We realise we must now rewrite those pages, not with the old, familiar words, but with new words that are forming in our mind; new 'adventures', often quite different from anything we knew before.

We no longer know how each chapter; each page in this *Book of Human Life* is going to end. The outcomes that we once knew and kept re-reading and repeating have vanished. Some people may try to re-write the words that they still remember from centuries, but the stories no longer seem credible or believable.

However more and more people are looking at those fading pages and beginning to realise that within their heart is an author who is easily capable of writing a new *Book of Life;* a book with much more beauty, with words that flow with beautiful poetic nuances. There may even be illustrations that just seem to appear in lovely vibrant or translucent colours.

As we begin re-writing our *Book of Life* we also realise that the wisdom we are creating will not remain imprinted for centuries, it will also fade and leave blank pages to be re-written by other new authors. As we write over the fading pages we know that the more beautiful our new creation, the more amazingly beautiful will be the works of later authors.

So although a gradually decreasing group of people are trying desperately to re-write the fading words of the old book with the same stories they have remembered, even as they write, the words continue to fade. They attempt to teach their younger children *the way things are and will always be,* but within the hearts of these young people are also authors with greater abilities, who will eventually want to re-write the old history into new, more beautiful stories.

The *Book of Human Life* is no longer that book of ancient history; it is being re-written day by day with words from the heart, stories of love, compassion and oneness......and we are the new authors.

Following a New Map

Please note that the map you are following may also have been written in other very different times. You might be listening to advice from previous more primitive sources, and even though we have been taught that this direction must be followed for our survival, the map may now be out of date,

There is an up-to-date and current map that has been written for us to follow. Where is it? It's not written on perishable paper, nor is it recorded within electronic devices; it's in a far safer and more secure place – it is recorded within our heart.

Are we able to read heart-recorded information? Where can we go to learn a course in this language? Surely we can Google it? No, but it can be learned through meditation; quiet listening to our inner self. This information would not have been recorded within us if we were unable to retrieve it.

The new map is recorded within the hearts of every person on our planet and is *readable* in any language because it is recorded in the language of love, compassion, wisdom, and peace. However you will need the desire to uncover it, and then have faith that what you are receiving is *real*. When you follow these new messages you will soon be able to discern whether they are coming from the heart, or still from the old, outdated map.

Each new child born on this planet receives the newest, most updated copy. Those people with the old information may attempt to rewrite this new wisdom back into the more primitive information with which they were taught.

However within these young ones is recorded far more wisdom than the older people may be able to understand. So do not try to direct them onto the pathway that you were taught was the only one to follow.

Ask them for suggestions; help them to access this new wisdom, then watch and wonder as far more beautiful pathways emerge from the wilderness.

The creation of these pathways is perfectly aligned with the new maps. Listen; watch; learn; follow, and enjoy.

Receiving Information

One very important process during this human life is the receiving of information. I often mention the value of intuition and noticing synchronicities.

Consider that this new *Book of Life* is written as an information manual; it contains steps we could follow, and new information is written on each page.

When we live our lives expecting each day to be much the same as the previous one, and not expecting anything new or different, then this is what we will receive. Our *receptors* are set the same as the day before, the previous week, the previous month. So although there is new and different information written each day, we don't see it.

When we realise that this life is a gathering of information to be assessed, studied, and then written into the journal of our life journey, we will begin to notice the many seeds of knowledge and wisdom scattered throughout each day.

Create an affirmation to assist with your awareness; for example;

"My inner ears and eyes are open and receptive to all messages which will increase my wisdom and understanding."

Begin each day speaking the affirmation and repeat it often throughout the day. You will find that many things you hear and notice may take on a new meaning.

It's as if we are turning new pages in this wonderful book we are reading, and each page seems different and much more interesting.

Even when emotions of sadness and annoyance imprint across our day they now have a new meaning, not just *"I'm feeling lousy"*, but perhaps *"now I understand why I was so hurt by my friend's comment; it reminds me of a childhood incident which I realise is no longer relevant."*

We have many helpers in Spirit – much loved friends and family who are living in a very different vibration.

We can't see them with our human eyes, but they are always close, wishing to help without infringing our personal development. They can scatter gifts of knowledge along our path, but only *we* can pause and notice these gifts and then ask for understanding. Only *we* can incorporate them into the book of wisdom we are writing and recording within our hearts.

No matter where you live, or how you are spending this day of your human life, if you are receptive to hints of wisdom and learning you will find them, often where you least expect.

Information I bring, both ancient and new;
Amazing wisdom, heart-centered and true.

Synchronicities

As we continue our life journey, everything may feel *same old, same old* on a physical level day after day. However there is another life happening alongside our everyday one. This life is not developing in time frames of *day-by-day*. As we achieve small changes towards compassion and harmony, that we may not even notice, the *other life* is growing beside and within us. As it continues to grow it will begin to silently change our every-day life.

We'll begin to notice little synchronicities – *"that's funny; I've been thinking about a friend I haven't seen for ages – and then she rings!" "I heard about a book I might enjoy, - there it is on sale!"* At first we will notice these synchronicities and think *"how strange was that"* but as they become a regular component of our life we might cease to even notice them.

Please don't allow that lack of attention. Notice them and give thanks. Perhaps these so-called synchronicities are Spirits way of saying, *"look how much closer you are becoming to your actual inner being?"* Always notice synchronicities and allow them to grow, expand their influence and become an important part of your human day-to-day life.

Your life no longer seems *same old, same old;* there are little touches of magic. The synchronicities may seem like magic because they are not part of the expected and usual life path you've always followed, when the only unexpected events were those of drama and fear. Notice that as these little synchronicities arrive they also touch your heart with a little *"Oh my God that was wonderful,"* a touch of joy and warmth.

Whenever I lose something, I always ask the *Little Being who Finds Things* to find the missing object and place it where I'll see it, regardless of where I might have lost it. Amazingly the lost object always appears, lying in a very obvious place where I had searched, and where it certainly wasn't before! I don't know how this happens, and it doesn't seem to matter whom you ask – *Little Being*, or *St Anthony* etc. I'm sure you've had similar experiences.

When my partner lost his hearing aids, we searched the house, especially around the computer where he often works. We moved everything off the desk, even the keypad. A short while later we returned and there were the hearing aids sitting in front of the computer on the empty desk!

Recently I discovered one large silver earring was missing. When I asked for its return, a voice in my head said to go to the park where I'd walked the dogs that morning, and look under a specific tree. Sure enough, there was my earring sitting upright on some grass!

Understand synchronicities as little signposts showing that we are following a new path of love and compassion; we are becoming closer to our real inner being, a part of the creative God-force of the universe. The Inner Life that has been growing silently is beginning to meld with our human life. This is happening gradually so there is no fear; *"Oh what is happening to me, I don't feel like myself!"*

As you gradually uncover your *Inner Spiritual Self* you recognize that it's your real, actual self which you have always known, but have stored away while concentrating on your human ego journey. Understand the synchronicities as little reminders of the wonderful *Spiritual Being* that has been hiding beneath your human clothing. Welcome each synchronicity and wait joyfully for the next one to be created.

Synchronicities point to where the Light shines;
I follow them, they're my guiding signs.

Following the Flow of Our Heart

With the new insights, tools and wisdom we are now receiving comes a challenge. What are we going to do with these? How do we intend to use them? Will they just sit waiting within, perhaps being delegated to our unconscious memory, so our life journey can continue without any new challenging experiences?

Or will we examine these new tools and decide to use them to create a more harmonious and compassionate life?

These new abilities and wisdom go beyond our recent memories of other life journeys on this planet. Every small experience we encounter can now be seen in a different light; our response can be in harmony with the higher dimensional energies of love, kindness and compassion.

We may look at the written texts we have followed in the past but they no longer seem so relevant. Instead of an old dictionary of words and meanings, it's as if we have been given a new alphabet and now need to create our own words. It sounds impossible, but it's not; as soon as we start, new words and meanings will begin to flow from our heart.

With the new energy may come the possibility of change; perhaps a different career or hobby, or perhaps a different aspect of our current position may now be seen.

There will always be those who attempt to draw us back into our old mold, but we resist them easily, calmly with no disruption or conflict.

So whether your life path takes a new direction, or finds a more inspiring path through familiar surroundings, there will be a different feeling, perhaps initially ungrounding, and you may miss the familiarity of the past. This is when you will need the qualities of faith and trust; listen to your inner guidance, go with the flow of your heart.

We now realise that every decision we make, be it ever so small, must be in harmony with this flow. The flow of peace, love and kindness is the energy that is gradually changing the planet.

Writing Words from the Heart

There is something which I suggest you continue to remember. It is the power of the written word. I don't mean texting, or even typing on the computer or laptop. When we pick up a writing implement and paper and write from our heart, the words have far more power than we may realise, and the energy of the written word spreads much further than we understand.

The act of thinking and writing creates an energy which does not disappear when the page is closed, so it's important to write words from our heart. The legibility is not important; it is the thought, the action and the intent that creates the energy. Do not write negative words of fear and anger; much better to write words of forgiveness for any negative thoughts. Remember, even if you decide to destroy your writing, the energy continues.

I still remember a situation where two of my friends were having a dispute. One friend wrote a handwritten letter to the other complaining about what had upset her. The friend receiving the letter decided to secretly burn it, a common practice at the time. However the friend, who had written the letter, not knowing it was being burned, rang me to say she was feeling as if her body was on fire! When they each understood the consequences my friends resolved their differences.

However words and symbols written with love still carry the same energy that can be felt even when the language is not understood.

When I post out Shell Essence newsletters to customers who prefer to receive the hard copy, I always focus on that person, and write a little message on the back of the envelope. I receive a lot of gratitude for those little hand-written messages.

Create your writings in a peaceful environment, and with the intent to create beauty and harmony, and this will prove to be as powerful as the spoken word.

Handwriting contains an energy that goes much deeper than the words themselves; much as a painting contains the artist's intent, as well as the energy of colours and patterns.

There is another language enfolded within the creativity of art and writing that is read by the intuition; it speaks to the inner self on a level not readily understood by the ego self. This is the energy that is underlying all our planetary existence and must never be lost, but which will become more easily understood as our awareness continues to grow.

All forms of creativity express this energy-language that should be recognized as an important communication. It's difficult to explain that which we call *energy*; it's the invisible sea in which everything is immersed, yet everything is also part of. When we give intent to create something, this pulls from the *sea of energy* the strands that will swirl together to create the pattern of our intent. When we write our intent as well as speak the words, the strands become more defined and eloquent. It is within this invisible sea that we are creating our lives – our experiences, our awareness, and the material forms of our creativity.

From this moving swirl of colours and patterns we are creating our work of art that is our human life.

Love, gratitude and grace
Open doorways to a better place.
New beginnings offer more
Trust, and enter the open door.

The Importance of Questioning

Even though I have written many times about the difference between ego-based and wisdom-based desires, you may not always understand the difference. Always question; ask for the intuitive wisdom that lies within your heart, whether this idea, concept or action is for your highest benefit. Listen to the immediate response, and follow its advice.

As we continue to question instead of always accepting, our inner wisdom will continue to grow and expand until we merge with this wisdom. Then ego-based desires will be seen only as nuisances tapping on the closed door of our mind that will no longer automatically open for them. Question everything; not in a competitive *"I am right and this is wrong"* ego mind-set, but with an open *"I wish to know more"* request.

When we begin to question long-held beliefs we may be surprised to discover that they have been built not on a firm foundation of spiritual knowledge or science, but on *shifting sands*. The more we question, the further we will be able to advance our current wisdom and knowledge.

CHAPTER 3

❖

DISCOVERING AND RECOVERING WISDOM

For ages we thought that life follows a plan
That we must all obey, as best as we can.
Then one day it hits us; this just can't be right!
It seems we've learned nothing but conflict and fight!
There must be a better way; aren't we designed
To have care and compassion, and not just resigned
To repeat those old patterns for ever and ever?
We could sort out these problems if we just got together.
So lets think more deeply; lets all have a say,
Observe what we've learned, and are learning, each day.
The wisdom is there – we just need to grab it!
And make kindness and peace our new human habit.

A problem facing many people today is a lack of wisdom. Even though we know there are more valuable ways of solving our problems, especially those which involve other people, we often fall back into old patterns of conflict and of *right* and *wrong*.

When meditating, relax and ask for more wisdom – by wisdom I am referring to the connection with heart-centered, intuitive knowledge, then new ideas can gradually flow through.

There has been much wisdom planted on Planet Earth that is now available for all. Once, only gurus and those who were called wise men and wise women were able to access this wisdom, but now the only problem which is preventing anyone from accessing it is a closed mind – closed by choice!

The wisdom that has been downloaded onto our planet has been planted within the vibrational magnetic energy grid to which we are all connected. Therefore it is available to anyone who chooses to access and use it for the highest benefit of all. Those who would use the knowledge for harm or for ego-centered purposes will not choose to access it. As enough people are open to new, more compassionate ideas, they will discover them.

This is already happening, and on a larger scale than we may currently realise. Perhaps we don't always see how this knowledge is being used, but we will notice that many people are thinking differently. Instead of *"nothing will change; this is the way life has always been,"* they are thinking *"there must be a better way to handle this situation."*

In the past, like-minded people could only connect within their village, community or perhaps country; now they can easily connect world-wide and this is happening. When we search for world-wide compassionate caring actions we will find them; then we can join these caring communities if we choose.

Learning Lessons

As you continue moving through your life you will notice there are many things you had always accepted that you now begin to question, or wonder why? Although you only see hints of the *big picture,* the more hints you see, the more questions arise. You must understand that to make this human life possible, there must be lessons which are easily learned.

These lessons, these experiments in living harmoniously with others, are learned by experiencing the results of behaving in different ways. Once learned, we remember them; they are stored in our unconscious mind, or cellular memory, and we have no need to repeat them. However we may watch others still experimenting and learning the results of those actions.

Look at the wars being fought on our planet at present. Many people see this course of action as stupid and pointless, but those involved in wars are still learning lessons and making choices; *"what will happen if I do this? Or what will be the result if instead I behave this way?"* Those who have already learned the lessons of warfare in previous lifetimes remember that fighting each other is pointless; it doesn't create peace or harmony.

There are many lessons being learned as we walk our present life path. If we have previously learnt the lessons of warfare we won't need to experience these again. However there are more subtle lessons toward creating harmony, within families, workplaces or relationships. Although physical weapons are no longer an option, emotional weapons are just as harmful, decisions must be made regarding their use.

Bullying is a lesson confronting many at present and sometimes only by experiencing the results of this behaviour can decisions be made whether this creates harmony and oneness, or whether it does the opposite. Those who are using the weapon of bullying, or experiencing the results of being bullied, are learning this lesson.

What lessons are you currently experiencing? Perhaps developing self esteem and belief in your innate abilities? Are you permitting yourself to learn new skills? Or are you avoiding these?

Your journey will confront you with many lessons. Once learned you may never need to confront those issues again.

Receiving an Upgrade

We do not really understand our life and our many life-journeys. It's difficult to describe in concepts that can be understood. That is why I often talk in pictures or parables as they were once called. However when we realise there is much more to our lives than material sustenance, new wisdom and awareness will overcome the limited beliefs and understanding we have lived with until now.

So firstly, look at your surroundings; can you understand they are illusionary? They are created by a 3D energy and this was all that could be drawn with our *3D brush*. But now some are able to explore further; there is higher frequency energy available. Even when you can't see, or vision differently, you can *feel* the difference. However it is often difficult to believe that there is more to life than our very long journeys in 3D illusion have permitted us to understand.

Although we see the same surroundings that we have always seen, somehow, in some vague way, they are different. This can make us feel a little ungrounded, but please persist; we are due, in fact overdue, for an *upgrade*. It can only happen if we allow this slow transformation, and as we say *go with it*.

The signs that the *upgrade* is beginning is when the same human activities keep happening around us, but they don't seem as *real* as they once did; we feel somewhat detached from them. They don't have the same effect; instead of viewing negative events with distaste and even fear, we see confused, suffering people who appear to know no other way of dealing with their pain and anger. Instead of feeling distaste and condemnation we feel compassion. The more we become aware of the subtle changes and accept them, the more *higher reality* can be offered us.

Yes, it's a slow process when measured in human time, yet the *upgrade* has to be set in an apparent slower time frame so we can adjust to it. In actuality it's progressing beautifully.

Changing Perspective

Even though our life journey seems a day to day, month by month journey, it's actually an unfolding of our *Spiritual Being*. In this terminology *spiritual* doesn't mean *religious:* it describes the *infinite energy of love* which is dressed in a human body.

As we start to gradually unfold our true and *Infinite Being*, we will begin to detach from our physical, material life. Relationships, and the planetary energy of nature will still be important, but other details of our life may lose some of their significance.

As our *Spiritual Being* begins to unfold, we realise our true power over the physical 3D life; then many things will take on a different perspective.

This may occur so slowly we won't really notice the change until we look back at our earlier life. The unfolding must be gradual and barely noticeable, so we don't become anxious and wonder if we're mentally unbalanced! We need to be comfortable with our different outlook on life. There will probably be times when we are amazed by our wisdom – *"where did that knowledge come from?"*

A potential problem may arise if we temporarily slip back into our old habits and berate ourselves *"I should have known better!"* Instead of feeling disappointed, congratulate yourself because you can now see that behaviour in a different light, and not want to perpetuate it.

Another problem that might trouble us is the different perspective from which others are creating their lives. It's not easy to remain centered and non-critical now we understand the higher ethics of compassion and forgiveness. However every circumstance that triggers our attitude of *"why can't they see what they're doing?"* is a lesson in non-judgment for us.

Even when our current life seems less exciting, we can use this time to cement our personal growth. Know that as we develop more spiritual wisdom in our everyday lives, this energy is gradually helping those around us. We may meet some conflict as others try to emphasize their views and deny ours, but again, we can remain firmly consistent, peaceful and forgiving.

If you're unsure how to respond to difficult situations, ask your *Inner Self.* Trust the guidance you receive. If there's still confusion, meditate, as this will help clear the mindless chatter, and allow your own wisdom to flow.

Take note of the situations you now face with a smile and peaceful demeanor, which once would have triggered an angry response. Know that even when your physical 3D life seems to be continuing without noticeable changes, your spiritual energy is unfolding with amazing abilities developing.

Trust and Obey

There is one message that is of major importance in the lives of all those who are trying to steer a path of love and beauty through the waves of dissent. It is to *trust and obey.*

Obey your intuitive thoughts and dreams. If you have a wish and desire to create a life of abundance in the realm of beauty and love, to give assistance to those whom you perceive to be in need, then follow your heart.

We may not always see where that path is leading, but if it is taken with trust, and a desire to create love; if we have a positive energy of fearlessness and balance, then that is where our path will lead.

Perhaps the most difficult of all the lessons we are learning is to trust. When we try to steer our life with trust towards a positive outcome, the ego mind, which is always directed by fear, may attempt to hold us back, or turn us towards a different direction. Realize that you may be programmed by a belief in lack, or by a fear of other people's reactions. This fear is directing the movie you are creating. A lesson all parents should teach their children is that their thoughts and beliefs create their lives.

So an important lesson is to connect to the messages our *Inner Intuitive Self* is constantly sending us; listen, trust, and learn. Differentiate between the inner messages from the heart, and the ego-based thoughts of fear and distrust.

I still remember a time when my teenage son was catching a train home late at night. I told him I was worried about his safety; I had heard of gangs causing serious trouble on the late night trains. His reply was that nothing dangerous would happen to him because he had a positive attitude, but with an attitude of fear like mine, anything might happen to him! Of course he was right! I made a conscious effort to replace my fear with trust.

The birds in my garden expect and trust that seed will be put out for them. They are right. I hear their calls and can't ignore them!

When we ask our *Inner Self* with trust, and an open mind we will receive a quick answer before the ego mind has a chance to weigh in with all the doubts and fears.

Please make a habit of asking your *Inner Self,* not just asking, but obeying!

The task for humanity is to create a planet of loving support for all. Trust – and obey your intuitive heart.

The Ability to Receive

Another quality we will need to develop for our present life journey is the ability to receive. Many of us have no difficulty in *giving;* we've always believed in the value of giving to others, whether material gifts, money to charities, birthday or special presents. Perhaps *giving* makes us feel important; an unconscious *better than* – when we give we feel abundant, or we're *doing the right thing.*

But receiving? That may be a different story. Receiving may stimulate an unconscious *"I don't deserve." "I'm not good enough;"* a feeling of low self-worth. For some reason we find receiving more difficult than giving.

So we may turn our backs on the many gifts and wisdom offered to us because of an unconscious feeling of not being worthy or deserving. This unconscious belief probably comes from a family-tree history of belief in lack and unworthiness, from childhood issues, or even from other lifetimes, particularly if those lives were spent in religious institutions where lack was believed to be spiritual. So while consciously we may tell ourselves, *"yes, I deserve this gift; I acknowledge this wisdom,"* an unconscious feeling of *"no, I can't accept"* blocks our ability to receive.

Instead of denying this inability to receive, acknowledge the difficulty, thank it for the important position it may have held in the past. Then imagine you are opening the door of your unconscious mind, bidding farewell to this negative belief, welcoming in the gift of receiving. Remind yourself that you are part of the wonderful energy of creation; there is no lack because everything for your highest benefit is entering that open door, and you are welcoming it in. Every gift, every word of praise, every word of wisdom is welcomed with gratitude and received with love, because you are the generator as well as the receiver.

Imagine you are a beautiful garden. When the sun shines, the flowers open to receive the light, to give their pollen and nectar, the bees are welcomed. When rain falls does the soil refuse to accept it? Or do the roots drink the rain with gratitude; the leaves open and the garden flourishes? All of nature both gives and receives. When we receive with love and gratitude we can also spread the joy and peace we are receiving.

Words and Thoughts

Perhaps we have lost belief and faith in the importance of words and thoughts? However our words, our thoughts create our lives. They are both connected; our thoughts influence the words we speak, our words send patterns of thoughts that create our actions. When we become conscious of the words we speak – even in jest – we will begin to notice how they are manifesting in our lives.

If we listen to our *Inner Self,* our intuition, we hear only positivity and love; but our ego-driven thoughts are often those of anger, fear and resentment. These angry, fear-driven thoughts will create words of anger, fear, and the expectation of difficulty. So guess what our lives will be manifesting? Those listening to our negative words may take them on board and spread them further.

However it's usually the silent conversations we have with ourselves that cause the most damage. If we listen with attention to the words and thoughts with which we often silently deride ourselves, understanding that our ego-selves are listening and then attempting to create what they hear, we might take more care.

Remember everything is vibration; words of love and positivity create vibrations of harmony that spread throughout our physical bodies and our auras and thus create health and happiness. Words of fear and anger create negative vibrations that impact our bodies, and the lives of those around us.

The *bottom line* of our words is our thoughts. These are often unconscious records and memories of damage from childhood, other times, or negative events which have impacted us. When we can't control these damaging thoughts, we can change them with positive affirmations that we need to speak aloud and repeat often.

So when you wish to change your life, change your thoughts, your words. Listen with wisdom; decide if what you are saying and thinking is creating happiness and peace, or are you actually describing what you don't want?

Your thoughts are your building materials and words are your tools. Are you building an old run-down house with ancient rotting timber and broken bricks from long ago, using rusty, damaged tools? Or are you creating a beautiful home with lovely, strong, harmonious materials and with the ease and grace of modern equipment? The choice is yours.

The Eternal Inner Being

Although we are often focusing on what is changing in our world or in our lives, there is something which will never change; that is our inner, eternal, *Spiritual Being*.

The changes we're experiencing in our human lives, and seeing in the lives of others, are floating upon a background that is our eternal and indelible *Inner Self*. This *Inner Self* will never change, despite what might be happening around us and appear to be impacting us.

Yes, we may feel the environment changing emotionally and physically as our cellular body struggles to implement a different energy vibration. However the inner *Eternal Being* which has always been our invisible core of wisdom remains unchanged. It's part of the universal energy of love with which the universe was created.

Some people are becoming aware of this inner core; however the awareness can only develop when there is trust and faith, as the amazing abilities of our *Inner Being* are not able to be fully observed in the energy with which our world is presently immersed.

Despite what we see happening around us as humanity struggles to learn new methods of survival and growth, know that the inner core is not affected by this. So whenever you experience problems and negative attitudes impact you, do not lose faith and trust; please remember that nothing can touch your *Inner Being*, your inner core of love and compassion, that has abilities beyond our present comprehension.

This *Inner Being* has been discovered by many great people throughout our history when they were deluged by incredible negative events. Instead of taking the easy path and succumbing to these events, they maintained a strength of belief and purpose that may have seemed impossible. They connected to the strength of their *Inner Being* of love, compassion, and peace that changed the negative events into peace, and harmony. This then changed the lives of many people.

This powerful *Inner Being* dwells within us all, but after many centuries of seeing mainly the external ego qualities, we have often lost faith in that which we really are.

Allow the external changes to continue, but hold tenaciously to the wisdom held within your Inner Spiritual core.

Wisdom and Knowledge

There is so much spiritual help available during this lifetime on Planet Earth, however much of this cannot yet be understood; our wisdom and creativity must arise from within, not from Spirit attempting to explain.

Heart-centered wisdom and creativity are of much greater value than knowledge. These will rise to the surface when there is a strong impetus to change or correct something. Unfortunately the impetus often has to be very strong before we decide *"I can't stand this any longer; there has to be a better way!"* Then, miraculously we often see a solution. This will even happen on a world scale when we eventually tire of conflict, competition and separation to solve our current problems.

Wisdom is the *stitching* with which we are all created; the underlying core of our humanity. Wisdom is connected to the heart, so whenever we lay aside our human ego-self and connect instead to the heart, wisdom is waiting.

Wisdom will not necessarily show us how to create more environmentally friendly energy for example, but will show us that a better solution is possible. It will point to a door that has been closed for many centuries. Then we must open the door and decide what we can now envisage and invent.

The solutions to all our current problems lay waiting for us to use our wisdom, to acknowledge there are problems, and give intent to solve them.

Wisdom helps us to see things differently, then we can choose to make a change. Knowledge will gather together all the current information we have already discovered, to help find the solution. With wisdom shining its rays of heart-centered *Light* we will then create solutions of value with no harm; solutions that will solve problems, rather than solve one problem but create another.

In your day-to-day life when you confront any problem that may seem to be insurmountable, use meditation techniques to connect to your heart and access the wisdom within. Wisdom will show us a different way to view our problem, and once wisdom, intent and knowledge join hands we will find that the problem is already solved.

Wisdom I bring
Both ancient and new.
Higher vibrations
Lay waiting for you.

CHAPTER 4

RECOGNISING AND ACCEPTING CHANGE

When we look to nature, we see a world of change,
Everything adapts, it's not considered strange.
Change is the healing that helps all things grow,
It's part of nature's natural energy flow.
Change is also an asset for us.
If we change our direction without fear or fuss,
We might avoid repeating a previous error,
Even though we may often step forward with some terror!
But change is a blessing we all need to accept;
Our lives would be boring if change we reject!
We might never know what wonders await,
Till we step forward with courage, and begin to create.

As each year passes, higher dimensional energy is being gradually down-loaded onto our planet. As we absorb the previous *particles* we are able to down-load more. We will only notice these changes if we look back to the way we were, and become aware of the differences we can now observe. We may see these as blessings – but more likely as difficulties!

So when you become aware of difficulties – actions, ideas, and changes of which you disapprove, please don't allow your response to be unhappiness and despair. Realise that noticing these is the first step towards changing them. Noticing what is not in harmony with love, peace and compassion is taking a step higher on that ladder leading to peace.

29

The next step is creating the change. This is happening. A few drops of rain are often the prelude to a downpour, and downpours create rivers that can bring new growth to large sections of countryside. The small drops of positivity are so important for eventually creating rivers of peace.

Turning a New Page

We have been accustomed to staying within the narrow rut of creativity that was always available, and in which we were expected to continue. But soon we will observe that this narrow, well-worn track is only one of many branching off into different directions.

Once there seemed to be very little choice; we followed the path of expectations laid down by parents, grandparents, family and friends. Sometimes it worked and was enjoyable, or at least satisfying. Sometimes it felt like chains holding us down, but even if it felt uncomfortable, we knew we were doing the 'right thing'.

Now we have turned a page, there is a new map with many roads to many different outcomes; they all begin at our feet. What should we do? Should we follow the one our parents would approve?

When I finished Secondary school my mother expected me to do Nursing or Teaching, as *"that is what girls do."* However I decided to study Occupational Therapy, an occupation then very new to Australia, and one not many people seemed to know about. (I had seen one small brochure; however that was all the information I needed.) I was accepted, and managed to receive a commonwealth scholarship which paid for my fees and part of my accommodation.

I followed this path very happily for a number of years, then another path opened, and then another, each with different experiences and learning.

There are many paths we may be *expected* to follow; for example we should have a university degree regardless of how much expense is involved, and whether our heart is open to the experience, or only our ego mind.

It's so important to follow our heart's desire, rather than the influence of family or friends. *The way things have always been* will not create a future of wisdom, creativity, and accessing the high ideals of spiritual growth and understanding.

New avenues of creativity that were once veiled in mist and fog are now becoming clear, and open to all those who allow themselves to envisage different paths, follow their heart and their intuition. Those still bound by the ropes of tradition and ancient beliefs will require much courage and faith to follow a different path, but each person who does so will create paths easier for others to then follow.

There are no failures; every thwarted attempt towards greater creativity still creates an energy of positive change.

Changing the Pattern of Conflict

There is something else of which we will need to be aware during these challenging times. We have lived many lifetimes on this planet. We have developed a pattern of behaviour from a long-standing belief in competition and fighting to resolve conflicts. Many of these patterns are repeating themselves as our lives continue to revolve around creating the same scenarios; these old solutions and responses have become *wired* into our unconscious memory. However when we confront the same situations with the same behaviour, no different responses can be learned.

As the patterns repeat they become more deeply imbedded. Yes, cultures have changed, appearances have altered, and physical structures are different, but within these outer appearances the inner behaviors, expectations and methods of dealing with conflicts have remained virtually unchanged. That is, until now.

These writings keep emphasizing that there has been a change in the energy vibrations which are affecting much of our planetary life; *the way things have been* is not necessarily *the way things are.*

This change has now given us the opportunity to express our lives differently, but it will take some time before this becomes an easy option. We have been programmed for centuries with the belief in physical strength, power, and the importance of physical wealth to solve all our problems; therefore the rich and powerful have dominated our world.

We now have a choice to choose the old belief in physical power and strength, the importance of material goods, or instead the silent, innate power of peace, love, harmony, and interconnectedness. We will see this choice being played out on many levels, as individuals, groups and countries vie with each other for their concept of power – survival of the wealthiest and strongest, or a desire for peace and harmony.

However this choice is also confronting us in our daily lives. When we experience confrontation and attack, the instinct is to fight back. Can you overcome this basic instinct which is imprinted by fear; instead step back and consider the situation from a perspective of acceptance and peace?

Start with small, seemingly inconsequential situations and opportunities that arise within your business life and within family and friendships. Each time you stifle your instinct to confront and challenge, and choose instead a peaceful compassionate response you are changing the old energy one breath at a time. Each tiny individual energy change will be imprinted into the whole and cannot be destroyed. These small positive energies will raise our own vibration and place one more calming drop of love into the ocean of humanity.

Fear of Change

The *time of change* that we are constantly hearing about has been arriving for many of our human years. The planet is changing, but the change isn't catastrophic; it's a natural cycle. Cycles are something we are experiencing throughout our lives. The only danger or difficulty is our fear of what might happen, our fear of not being able to cope.

This current planetary cycle is a period of gradual change; only when we look back will we really see the major changes. This cycle is calling for new thinking; for the ability to become much more aware of what is changing in our environment, for us to make choices, and take action to implement these choices.

Choices regarding change will confront us each day in small ways that can be easily dealt with. We are learning to be adaptable; as we adapt to small changes in our lives, we will become able to adapt to bigger and more important changes. Because we have lived many lifetimes where we always knew what to expect, adapting to any change may now be quite uncomfortable.

Some groups of people are being confronted with very definite and even life threatening changes. These changes are lessons for all, not just for those directly involved. No longer are events in other parts of our world hidden from view and irrelevant.

Once we become aware of these events, even though we may not be personally involved, they will affect us. They become part of our mental environment, and bring up questions regarding how we might all cope.

These situations are our lessons in acknowledging changes and mentally adapting to them. We are no longer oblivious to what is happening on other parts of the planet; they are impacting us even though the events may be happening to a distant group of people.

Everything is imprinted into the energy of Planet Earth, and is being consciously or unconsciously read by us. This is the reason many are feeling uncomfortable at present. The change in vibrational energy has created a new form of *energy sensitivity*, where many people are aware of changes in their emotional environment and are reacting to this.

Yes, the waves of fear created by change will cause much discomfort until we learn to react with peace and trust. When these positive energy vibrations permeate our minds, then the cycle of change can continue to peacefully evolve and stimulate the creation of new solutions and inventions.

Coping with Change

Do not despair when clouds cover the blue sky; remember the blue sky is still there, it hasn't been destroyed by the clouds. Just wait until the clouds depart, as they always do, and find a way to occupy your troubled mind with a positive purpose until the clouds clear.

We live on an evolving planet, not a planet that never changes from day to day. We are also *Beings* who are uncovering our true reality. How boring, uneventful and fruitless would be a life that was always the same, day after day, with no changes, no challenges or chance of advancement. So honour your changing environment, your changing life. Do not look for and expect the worst scenarios.

We may never have walked this particular path before, so please don't try to push it into old remembered patterns. It is changing, and yes, that may sometimes be uncomfortable and self-doubt arises, but allow the new and wonderful to unfold.

Imagine that you are baking a cake; you need to put the mixed ingredients into the oven. If you leave them sitting in a bowl on the table, will the cake cook?

No, it requires the heat of the oven, a very different environment. Do you think the ingredients panic and say *"oh, what will become of us?"* No, they trust the baker to know exactly what she is doing; that the oven is the right heat, and that the cake will be removed at the right time. You are both the cake and the baker. You are evolving from a mixture of different ingredients into a beautiful cake. You will know exactly how to achieve this.

Do not panic that the planet is changing; we are perfectly capable of making the best use of these changes; it is not a disaster, it's just change. We will need to develop more trust, more faith in ourselves to cope with and make good use of the change.

A lot of what we see at present is created by those who are trying to reverse change back into *the way things were and have always been*. This is creating conflict with the new energy and will not be successful. When we realise that the changes within humanity and within our planet are irreversible, in desperation we will begin to open our minds to new possibilities, and then realise that actually, all is well.

The changes are progressing slowly, at a rate with which we can cope without too much fear. Do not look back *at the way things were;* this is what many are doing at present. look ahead at *the way things could be*. We can then create an amazing humanity with new discoveries and wisdom far beyond what many are allowing themselves to envisage today.

Unconscious Fears

When your life path seems a bit difficult, proceed carefully. There are always rough places on every journey, but they will not affect us when we walk with care; all lives will have difficult places and then smooth, comfortable sections again.

We may have companions who don't wish to move forward, who will try to stop us. When this happens, listen to their stories with compassion, but don't allow them to move you from your chosen path. Your kind words of encouragement could give them faith and courage to continue, however always remember that to continue or not is their personal choice.

Sometimes fear may cause an indefinite delay. Old unconscious memories from previous times may distort our belief in safety and the concept of being cared for. Do you have any old memories of fear that haven't yet been discarded? Are you aware of any old fears from previous lifetimes with an emotional pull, often when you least expect it?

When you notice the negative effects these fears have on others, perhaps you could pause, and become aware of any fears you may be inadvertently carrying yourself. Please don't just deny them or say *"I don't have to deal with that now, it's not really affecting me."* If these secret fears remain hidden and are not acknowledged and dealt with, they will gain greater power.

Perhaps you could create a ceremony to release them? Then find something of beauty to take their place? Perhaps you'll discover a crystal, or an attractive painting may catch your attention; something that will replace the fear with a sense of wonder, beauty and gratitude.

Do not berate yourselves if depression, discomfort, fears encroach again. Sometimes the decision to embrace a new way of being has to be made a number of times before the decision becomes permanent.

Now our life seems lighter without the weight of old fears and we continue on our way with a feeling of relief and lightheartedness.

The fears I've collected from my past,
I now bless, and toss away at last.
New growth of love and peace will spread
And fill that empty space instead.

Releasing Old Stuff

Your life journey will become more interesting when you realise how much you are changing and learning. Never in the course of our history has so much personal change been available for us. Many have taken the initiative and allowed the changes and growth.

No, it hasn't been easy; so much *old stuff* as we might call it, has arisen in our minds, emotions and thoughts to be released. Some have allowed themselves to become aware of the issues, then faced and released them. Others are still in denial and unable at this time to confront the negative issues; but when they are ready, the *old stuff* will arise again and continue to do so until they are prepared to release it.

We have all lived in more primitive times where we may have been treated very harshly, to the degree that this pain and fear has become imprinted into our DNA *Akashic* memory. These memories have been passed down to this lifetime when it is now appropriate to safely release them.

Many may have suffered severe punishment when they chose a different path to that which was permitted. These dim memories may make it more comfortable to deny the fear and pain that often arise seemingly spontaneously, but triggered by something or someone in our present life.

However when we release the emotions, the old memories will be cleared from our *Akash*. When we look at our world today we may see images of times long past being repeated, until the groups involved realise they are recreating from long ago.

What is actually growing and spreading at present is an influx of harmony and compassion at a greater level than has probably ever been seen and experienced on our planet. We are slowly creating a planetary energy where eventually all will benefit.

In the meantime continue learning and spreading your positive energy to all those with whom you connect. If negative events arise to threaten your sense of peace and harmony, see them as lessons and a chance for further growth. There is always another way of perceiving a situation. Search for the positive meaning and the positive lessons, then our inner wisdom will continue to develop comfortably and at our own pace.

Removing the Splinters of Childhood

In the events and happenings of our day-to-day life sometimes emotional issues will arise seemingly out of nowhere. We can't understand why we are feeling so despondent, depressed, perhaps angry or lonely. It doesn't make any sense, but the feelings are very real and poignant.

When seeking spiritual growth to activate greater wisdom and healing, what must first happen is for old, hidden, often denied emotional pain from childhood to be released. These forgotten memories may be blocking our life-paths, so to regain happiness and peace they must be released. However the first step is to acknowledge them.

If you have asked for healing and for wisdom, these old memories will rise to the surface. Please allow this to occur. Find some space in your busy life to acknowledge and identify the rather unpleasant feelings. Try to see them from a child's point of view. Feel the pain the child felt, and once you have experienced this aspect of your childhood or teenage years, allow it to melt away.

We cannot truly find the peace and happiness we seek while those old memories are still hiding in our unconscious. It's like having a deep splinter in our finger; each time we press in a particular direction we feel the pain, and it prevents us from carrying out that action. The only real relief is to remove the splinter. This is initially painful, but then our finger heals and we can use it again.

These old childhood memories are like splinters that must be removed, so allow them to surface. Yes, we will feel the child's pain, but we can also understand from an adult's point of view. Allow yourself to see how this particular splinter may have affected your life and prevented you from achieving some goals you may have wished to achieve, or perhaps avoiding some situations and experiences.

Now you have set yourself free, each splinter you release will mean less pain in the future, and therefore more freedom to explore different areas of possibility. When our intent is for healing, old negative influences from the past must be removed. Splinters not removed may fester.

Once the emotional splinter has been removed, dispose of it; perhaps by creating a ceremony which is meaningful to you? Each burden we release will create the space for peace, happiness and the freedom to be our true self.

Our Changing Landscape

When we are considering our life journeys on Planet Earth, we need to see them as voyages of discovery. Although our environment seems to be changing, please understand that this is planned, it is planned for our continual spiritual growth.

As you know, change is occurring. Do not fear planetary change; why should this appear fearful and disastrous? It is just change; as we continue learning and need new lessons to increase our knowledge and wisdom, so the planet is changing for, and with us.

When you see coral bleaching and animals disappearing don't view this as disaster. It's just change; a chance for new life to evolve. The media wishes to always show us death and disaster rather than change and new growth.

We may always make mistakes as we begin to try to deal with change, but didn't Einstein say: *"Anyone who has never made a mistake has never learned anything new"*?

Please walk with courage through your changing landscape, both internally and externally. When you see, or hear about planetary change, do not fear and expect disaster. It is change, and change brings new opportunities and learning.

As our external life is changing so is our internal life – our ability to heal ourselves, our ability to understand new concepts and ideas. Allow these new ideas to emerge and then test them – do they work for us, or are they just old information disguised?

Much new wisdom is awaiting. Change creates the impetus and opportunities as long as we don't see this as disaster and try to back-track into the way we have always known things to be. Notice how nature copes with change – new species evolve to benefit from the changed environment.

Each day look for an opportunity to create something differently; to observe something familiar and see it in a different way. Watch your thoughts with awareness to notice old repeating patterns, and then say to yourself *"but what if..?"*

'What if' allows your personal energy to flow in new and creative patterns, and you can use this energy in a freer and more expansive expression of life. Create an affirmation to welcome change and experience different solutions and paths.

> *"Dear Spirit, I am open and invite all new positive*
> *ideas and experiences into my life.*
> *I welcome change and learn from the opportunities it offers me.*
> *I am creating growth, harmony and a greater expression of love."*

Changing Energy Flow Patterns

Each day you will encounter people with different perceptions, opinions, and views of the world. Some will see only the negative, and as they watch and look for negative actions and events they will find them. Others with a more positive disposition may still be aware of the negative events, but will also observe many positive actions of love, caring and compassion; these are qualities they have programmed themselves to notice.

So every day we are actually creating our world, our lives and our interests by our beliefs and what we choose to notice.

Each life can be understood as a swirl of energy surrounding that person. When negative, fearful, uncomfortable actions are perceived, the swirl of energy becomes more rigid, less free and harmonious. Although this energy is attracted to other similar energies, it cannot flow harmoniously and freely; when the energies interconnect it's more a tying together.

However positive, heart-warming, happy expectations create swirls of energy that flow harmoniously with other similar swirls creating harmonious patterns complementing each other. Each individual person is contributing to the surrounding energy.

The different energy patterns formed by our beliefs, interests and perceptions are collected by experiences both within our present life and from previous lives. Even though a pattern has been formed it can be changed by our intent. Although these patterns influence our lives, we have control over how we envisage and change these aspects of our life.

If you decide to change a life of fear and doubt into one of contentment, peace and self-empowerment, try to surround yourself with friends who have those qualities. Search for contentment, peace and self-empowerment in your hobbies, your work-life, the internet etc. With intent and perseverance you can reprogram your thoughts and feelings, eventually redirecting your perceptions and expectations. Those who are sensitive to energy will feel the energy formations created by others and also by their surroundings.

If possible, spend some time in untouched nature; feel the resonance of harmony; try to create this same resonance in your home.

If you have no space for a garden, find room for plants in pots. There has been a lot of research to prove the positive energy change that potted plants bring to a work or living area.

With intent and awareness we can begin to change the slow tight energy of fear and self-doubt into the flowing harmony of peace and happiness. This will eventually spread those positive qualities to others around us.

Experiencing Change

Our life journey is now becoming very interesting. We are reaching *places* of which we have no memory; everything seems very different; change is certainly upon us. However the change is not how we have always expected and known it to be. Our surroundings remain the same as those we have always known, yet there is an unfamiliarity about them. They look the same to our human eyes, but they feel different. They seem to lose their intensity, their strong physical appearance, and now appear somehow luminous.

Everything is the same, but everything is also different. Some situations that once affected us strongly now have little effect, but other situations that would not have bothered us at all, are felt more deeply. Yes, something has changed along our human pathway, but what is it?

However there is no returning to *the way things were,* there is no *going back.* The direction we had been following has disappeared; there is nothing we can do but continue day by day, knowing that our intent will always direct us. What has changed is not our surroundings, but something within, it's a difference we haven't experienced before.

We notice we don't feel so fearful or anxious; somehow we are able to accept the changes. As we become accustomed to our new reality, *the way things were* becomes only a dim memory, almost like a dream.

We are no longer looking ahead for what might be further along the path, nor are we anticipating a final destination. Perhaps this is what *living in the now* is really like when we begin to truly experience the *now.* Instead of a combination of past, present and future, the *now* has nothing to do with time; rather it is connecting with more aspects of our multidimensional being.

So we continue our life journey, wondering if the changes we are experiencing *within* will lead to changes *without.*

However we begin to feel very peaceful and accepting, knowing that whatever we may need will manifest easily without effort or difficulty.

I am ready to change
And leave darkness behind
When I give my permission
God's Light I will find.

CHAPTER 5

OVERCOMING COMMON OBSTACLES

When you open your heart to the stuff which you've hidden,
Dark shadows arise, they're no longer forbidden.
They dance in the starlight; just look and observe,
And then please dismiss them, no more to be heard.
We've collected so many old pains and regret;
They need to be faced, forgiven and met
With love, reassurance they're no longer needed.
In our current life's work they shouldn't be heeded.
So open your heart now to new love and light.
Replace those old shadows with peace and delight.
Don't store away any more sadness and shame
To live in this life we accept, and don't blame.
Then when it's time to depart from this shore
We can join once again with those we adore.

Some people believe our planet is in dire trouble; they believe that humanity is going from bad to worse. This is not what is actually happening. Many people have already made a choice regarding the future of our planet, and the choice is not for destruction but for renewal.

Although the initial choice was to continue in the same well known cycle of war and destruction, the accepted way of life for millennia, there is now another choice, and enough people have made that choice for the balance to have shifted.

For a very long time our human civilizations have been involved in an old, tight circular rhythm of competition, fear and destruction. We can now see the pattern that has brought us to where we are today. Although a large number are still clinging to what they have always known – fight conflict with conflict – there are enough people on our planet who wish to change; who are looking towards peaceful coexistence, who want to resolve conflict with peace, togetherness and compassion. This will change the old cycles of destruction.

The first step towards change is to see what has been occurring. Those people still involved in conflict, both as victims and as perpetuators, are showing this in such a visual, confronting manner it can no longer be denied.

So now we observe the negative actions, we can place all our attention and inventiveness into creating solutions that will create harmony. These solutions can be as small and apparently insignificant as smiling at strangers; refusing to be drawn into arguments, refusing to take sides in personal conflicts. Each small act of kindness and compassion you initiate will help that energy build within another person, thus enabling harmony to begin and spread throughout our planet. When enough people make the decision to create peace and harmony, demonstrations of war and combat will no longer be necessary.

Please place all your attention upon deeds of kindness, and spread the awareness of these through our media. Use your electronic communications with others to spread stories of peace and happiness. You will then help to create communities of co-operation and harmony, so instead of forming *battle forces* we will then be forming *peace forces*.

Connect to your heart, allowing all your loving energy to be used to discover the amazing inventions that will change our lives and the lives of all on our planet.

Courage, faith and steadfast love
Will see you through
The stormy seas and shifting sand.
Stay firm and calm
We'll hold your hand.

Self-Doubt

You are travelling very well along your life journey; you have discovered changes and dealt with them; you have come across many trials and tribulations that you are learning to cope with, and not to give in or retreat back to darkness when everything seems to be approaching too fast.

But there is one lesson that, if missed we will need to address. That lesson is to love ourselves. We have a long history of believing in our unworthiness; we are not good enough. Even young children and babies may be scolded so many times they grow up believing in low self-worth.

We will never be able to achieve the spiritual growth we are seeking on this life journey until we can acknowledge – and more than acknowledge, know without any doubt that we are created with the energy of love we call *God*. We are a part of *God*. This concept must become more than mere words and intellectual understanding. It must grow within our heart until we know that the concept is true; we are a part of the amazing energy of love we call *God*.

Have you realized that the most difficult part of your journey may be your self-doubt?

Even when everything seems to be going fine; you notice the synchronicities and the beauty that surrounds you, yet you feel separate from it all. It's as if you are looking through a window and noticing the beauty, but somehow are not part of it.

Our greatest challenge on this life journey is to understand and feel our greatness. Every person on our planet is created from the vibrational energy of God. We can deny this knowledge and continue to use our power to create darkness, but when we realise that what we are is Light, everything changes.

Remember darkness is only the absence of Light; we can choose to close our eyes to our Light, but no matter what we do on our human journey we cannot destroy this Light, nor can any other person destroy our Light.

This wisdom is what we continue to seek, but seek no more. Stop; let the knowledge of our actual reality wash over and through you.

Each time self-doubt raises its ugly head and you question your worth in the grand design of everything, and begin to shrink into unworthiness, repeat these words over and over:

"I am that I am, immortal, eternal, universal and infinite. I am part of the God force that is creating the universe. I am love; I am compassion; I am part of the oneness of all."

Can you feel the wonderful loving energy of compassion, kindness, love, and beauty? What you are sensing is yourself.

The Distraction of Drama

As you continue forward on your life path many dramas may unfold and you might choose to take part in these distractions. Any drama is just that; a distraction, so rather than join sides to support or combat it, just bypass the drama, and send thoughts of love and compassion to those involved in it.

If the drama begins to impact you, step aside; do not allow your life to be distracted by this event. Our media is gaining much support from our unconscious addiction to drama. However if some negative dramatic event confronts us personally it's more difficult to remain detached; the negativity may trigger previously unconscious memories from other times where similar or even worse events unfolded around us, old fears arise to haunt our life. Again, just send thoughts of love and compassion and continue to move forward.

Now you have a chance to contemplate, forgive, and wipe off these old inappropriate memories from the blackboard of your mind. Do not allow this distraction to turn you aside from the path you have decided to take; the path that leads to the Light and to an evolved planet.

Wrap yourself in a cloak of compassion; listen to the stories of those suffering from negative actions; treat them with love and kindness, but do not join in their unhappiness, do not carry their energy on your life journey. If you continue to carry the many tales of suffering and pain you hear, their weight will impact your life with negativity you cannot resolve.

It is an art to listen, send love and support, but not to take on the misery of others.

Rather become a signpost pointing towards a life of peace and harmony that others will see and perhaps decide to follow.

Lack of Commitment

The quality of commitment is so important today as we are constantly distracted by the many different occurrences in our daily lives.

We need to be committed to the principles that are of greatest importance to us; perhaps the development of our inner wisdom; compassion; creating a loving relationship; releasing fear and developing inner peace.

We can so easily be distracted by our thoughts that then generate our actions. We might think *"Oh no, I won't bother with that today; I don't need to meditate again."* But once we allow our commitment to lapse it's not easy to regain it. When I commit to writing each morning before I start my day, I can keep writing. But when I think *"I'll just put it aside for today; one day won't matter,"* that day soon becomes a week, and it's not easy to start again.

So when you commit to create something of value – a better relationship; a deeper knowledge of your inner being; a morning meditation or walk in nature, don't allow the negative, lazy ego mind to distract you.

Commitment is belief in yourself, so even though the first steps may seem a bit difficult, as you continue with faith, trust and commitment, your creation becomes easier and more wonderful.

When we allow the distractions of life, or other people's beliefs to interfere with our commitment, we will lose our way, then something really negative may have to occur to redirect us toward the value of commitment again.

Commitment to the higher principles in which we believe, develops our strength of character, and will always help us to create an easier life path

What have you committed to today? Perhaps a healthier lifestyle? More exercise? Healthier food? No angry responses? Or perhaps a meditation to start the day?

Our commitment to a positive energy in whatever way seems most relevant to us, is another step higher on the ladder we are climbing towards reconnection with our wonderful, powerful *Inner Beings*.

Lack of Trust

Something important that we need to acknowledge, is our lack of trust in ourselves. There was a time long ago when we knew instinctively we were capable of making the right decisions for our lives to continue with abundance and positive health. But that was when *abundance* meant our needs would always be met.

Today we have been so programmed through fear that *day-to-day needs* now mean extra housing, a large bank account, loans, stocks and shares, *just in case.* When we don't have this accumulation of material wealth that our media may constantly tell us is necessary for future happiness, we no longer trust our ability to live a happy and productive life. We have lost faith in our inner wisdom and lost our belief that all will be well.

Many of our unconscious beliefs are being programmed into us by our media, and the media is becoming a large part of our lives. If we would spend part of every week with no radio, TV, computer or phone contact, perhaps we could start to believe in ourselves again, trust our innate ability to create a healthy, productive and fulfilling life. We have begun to rely on outside sources to tell us what to think, what to expect, and how to manage our lives.

When you rely on these media-based outside influences what do you hear? You hear fear.

Each day we are subtly programmed with more fear. We are shown fearful events happening in our world, even in our own communities. The unspoken message is *this could happen to you.* Much of our ill health has also been programmed into our expectations by constant exposure to fearful messages.

We have lost the knowledge that *we* are creating our lives; we have great and often untapped abilities to create an abundant, peaceful and happy community.

Please spend some time each day uncovering your creative, powerful being when the wrap of fear and powerlessness has been removed. You could create some space and time alone with yourself to listen to your own inner messages, regaining trust and faith in your own inner wisdom.

This is a wake-up call for us to realise the constant barrage of fearful messages we are receiving without giving any thought to our own, more positive beliefs. We are all capable of creating lives of peace and great creativity. Woven into the beautiful tapestry of nature and of our evolving planet are countless hints and examples of great wisdom and healing.

Please turn your backs on the illusions of fear; discover your trust, faith and wisdom.

Addiction to Material Abundance

One problem of which we all need to become aware is our concern for money – for material abundance. This is usually a constant worry in the back of our minds. *"Will I have enough money?" "How can I make more money?"*

When we relax, and become centered in our heart, we will see money for what it truly is – not a means of making us happy and trouble-free, but a material confirmation that our needs will be met. The confirmation we seek can only come from trust and faith in ourselves; when we have this self-belief our needs will always be met. But if we concentrate our thoughts on the belief in money to create happiness, to bring abundance and emotional security, we will probably find these missing. Become aware of what money means to you, and whether it really has the ability to create happiness and fulfillment.

When we can feel our self-worth, when we realise that we are an abundant and beautiful creation of the universe, our needs are automatically met. In fact we don't have any needs. We are a creation of abundance; so no matter what is happening around us in the world of illusion, we, a beautiful creation of the universe, are always in a state of abundance.

This is very difficult to comprehend; I can hear a lot of *"yes, but!"* However when we are centered in our heart, in our connection to all creation – not just our ego beliefs, a very different *feeling* arises within us. We now move through our human life attending to all the human concerns that are part of our 3D environment, yet we are no longer a part of them. We realise we are part of something much grander, beyond human concerns, words and concepts, but something we can feel in our heart.

Our need for money becomes irrelevant; our needs are for love, companionship, harmonious relationships, and the intangible gifts of grace which are automatically delivered when we connect to the reality of whom we truly are.

How do you discover this magnificent being? Connect always to the *feeling,* the inner knowing within your heart. Begin to notice the magnificence of the universe which is always surrounding you beneath the overlay of your basic 3D energy environment.

Do not attempt to analyze and understand this, but allow the *feeling* to shine through. Learn to feel from your heart with trust, then your perceived needs for money will drift into irrelevance.

Powerlessness

An uncomfortable feeling that is arising in the minds of many is a feeling of powerlessness; *"I don't really know what I'm doing, or supposed to be doing."* This feeling arises from the separation from an old familiar energy, belief system and lifestyle, and from friends and family with whom you can't seem to connect any longer.

Search for others who are on your *wave length* and communicate with them, even if there are only one or two friends at present whom you consider in this category. Their connection with you and your connection to them will be grounding, even inspiring during this time.

The others? Connect when you can, but step away and don't attempt to explain your point of view when you see they can't understand. If you continue to spend time with a group of these people who haven't yet been able to accept the new energy, you may feel powerless and perhaps begin to doubt your own wisdom. Please don't allow this to happen.

It's as if you are a sign-post pointing towards a different direction to that which many have walked before. Your sign-post is very important, even if only to help the few who trust and dare to see a different energy landscape. There were many times in your past when trust was important, but never as important as now.

When you're feeling powerless and lost, this is when you need to trust in your own inner power. It will never let you down.

We don't know how long this *change*, this feeling of *what's going on?* will last; it may be different for each individual. But when enough people accept and embrace the different energy with trust and courage, then this positive flow will permeate all. It's a bit like adding more lights into the darkness; tiny as each light may be, together they make a difference.

So please don't discount your feeling of powerlessness; attempt to change it into acceptance and trust. Connect with any sources that give you belief and courage – like-minded friends, spiritual writings that touch your heart, and of course the beauty and wisdom of nature. Trust and obey your heart. The following affirmation may help during times of self-doubt

"I am that I am, immortal, eternal, and a
powerful part of the energy of God;
and what I am has beauty and strength within the Oneness of all."

Low Self-worth

A quality which I believe is sadly missing in many lives today is that of self-worth.

We have all been indoctrinated with *this is the way you should be, and if you're falling short of that, then you are not OK.*

Unfortunately the concept of *this is the way you should be* is often flawed; a learned pattern from previous times. As children we are indoctrinated with the picture of *right* and *wrong* that is often not relevant to the growing wisdom of many today.

Instead of allowing the growth of this new wisdom, we are often still stuck in the old belief of needing to suffer; we are somehow unworthy; if something flows easily, then it can't be right. Not only do we have an expectation of difficulty, we also believe we are flawed; *"of course I'm wrong; what else would I expect?"* This concept was often part of old religious teachings, but is sadly incorrect.

The correct and up-to-date wisdom is that we are created in the image of *God*, the Creative Force of the universe, but when our inner *dials* are set to low self-esteem, we are often unable to see, and appreciate the amazing beings we actually are. We are the creators of our lives; there is no right or wrong, just amazing flowing creations.

The belief in low self-worth is a concept we have learned and accepted. The belief in great self-worth can only be found within us; it can't be taught or told to us by others, as the old programming is so strong it overrides the inner truth. By learning to listen to the voice within – that silent inner knowing – we can overcome the preaching of our outer, ego self.

Within each of us lays incredible wisdom rising to the surface. It's as if we've been painting our lives in grayscale when within us is an unlimited set of beautiful coloured paints and brushes just waiting until we can recognize and accept the wonderful artists we actually are.

But what if we are already painting our lives with these beautiful colours, but seeing only grayscale? An affirmation I like to use is:

"I am that I am, almighty, eternal, universal and infinite, and what I am has beauty, strength, love and compassion."

CHAPTER 6

UNEXPECTED PROBLEMS

Sometimes we may look at our lives,
And everything seems to be smooth.
But bad feelings impact us; it just makes no sense,
There's discomfort which just doesn't move.
So it's time to think deeper, look further afield;
We don't live alone, in a box that is sealed!
We should look to the planets, the earth and the sun;
Our friends and our neighbours, could they be the one
We've collected this fear from? We just need to trace it;
If nothing shows up, it's our own! We must face it.
But is it this life, or a fear from the past?
Old shadows are rising to be healed at last.

Dispelling Negative Memories

There are many people at present troubled by the accumulation of old negative memories that are being triggered by current emotions, events and thoughts. However these emotional memories if not released can inhibit and discolour our present life. We need to understand that these emotional events may have their roots in other times, when we had to grapple with difficult situations.

In those life times many succumbed and allowed situations to impact them in ways they would not have tolerated today. So as these memories arise they trigger both the old fear and anxiety and also current guilt.

Even though we may not remember the actions of the ego personality that resided within us during those times, we might receive hints of what happened and our possible role in those events. Old emotions may then arise and be mixed with guilt and despondency.

Those who have lived many lifetimes on this developing and evolving planet have participated in many lessons. They have now learned to follow paths of compassion and harmony. Yet these old shadow memories from times of difficulty can bring unexpected angst, anxiety, despondency and guilt. Please see these for what they really are – ties that need to be released. Don't allow your current personality to own them; see them as shadows you are moving away from, and keep your eyes always on the light. These old, barely conscious memories can cause much despondency if we hold onto them.

The more you can become happily involved in your current life, the less relevant these dim shadows will appear. The more *good deeds* you can deliver to yourself and to others, the further that old negativity will fade. It does not belong in this era; those lessons were engaged in and learnt so there is absolutely no need to recall them.

Whenever you feel guilt, despondency, and vague anxiety that seems to have no relevance to your current life, do not allow those old shadows to hook into you. Remember, Light is stronger than darkness; search for some Light wherever you can find it; something to make you laugh; a heart-warming story; or a warm, loving connection with others. These will dispel the shadows.

As you are becoming more sensitive to energy you will also become more aware of negativity. Don't allow those old memories to pull you back into darkness that is no longer part of your current journey. Awareness is the first step to dispelling the *shadows*, then use your intent to search for and create Light.

Removing Imprints from Other Times

As we continue to create our present life we may find problems confronting us that can seem rather weird. We feel that something within us has changed, but the change has not been positive. It seems as if our personality is different in some way; perhaps emotional difficulties such as resentment, anger, jealousy, competitiveness, or fear seem to be over-shadowing our usual calm nature. What is happening?

As we move further into the higher dimensional energy, old negative memories that have been held as part of our DNA Akashic record from long ago are now being expelled from their hiding places within our cellular memory. They are rising to the surface. Please do not own them; their time has long passed and they are showing their negative faces to be removed so that the higher frequency vibrations can take their rightful place.

Natural therapists can help you to remove these old imprints; vibrational essences such as the Shell Essences can also remove them very rapidly. However the most helpful positive action is to understand that they have come from old, possibly very difficult times.

Forgive the personality you created back then; understand that those old lessons have been learned and you have now turned the page. Today your lessons are very different, and newer, higher vibrational energies are needed to gain expanded wisdom.

When your personality seems to have changed in a negative manner, and you find yourself thinking *"this is not who I am;"* no, it's not the role you are playing today. Seek help to remove this negative imprint which has uncovered its face to be recognised and released.

In my work with Shell Essences I have discovered that these *negative imprints,* that some people call *negative entities* are confronting many people today. A particular Shell Essence ('Necklace Nerite') which I rarely used in the past is now an ingredient in nearly every personal blend I make. This Essence removes negative imprints from the cellular memory.

Understand, recognise, and forgive, for we have all played many roles in other human lives, but have learned those lessons and have no need to repeat them.

Now it's time for a very new and wonderful adventure. Much wisdom, love, compassion, and knowledge are holding out their hands to us. Goodbye negative imprints! We are ready to move on.

Understanding Our Planetary Environment

When there are no obvious impediments affecting your life, but some things suddenly seem unexpectedly difficult, there may be planetary energies which are now not in line with your personal energy pattern.

We are always connected by flows of magnetic energy to the planets of our solar system. When these planets change their positions, there will be a change felt in our bodies, especially our emotions. This won't make any sense if we try to find qualities in our everyday lives to connect with the changes we feel.

Understanding energy flows from the universe was once considered vital information, but today we tend to refer only to medical information and news.

Those who study astrology can usually explain why we have these unusual emotional and physical imbalances that seem to appear *out of the blue*. There are also websites you can check. Always be aware of changes in your body, your life and your emotions. When something seems out of balance, and it's difficult to maintain your happy, peaceful life and normal friendly interaction with friends and neighbours, there may be a reason you haven't considered.

Those who are sensitive to energy changes will usually feel affected by planetary changes and also by solar flares and solar winds. So if there has been no underlying tension from difficulties in family relationships, workplace or health issues, you might need to look further afield. We are vibrational beings living within a universe of vibrational frequencies, so of course we are impacted by changes in our energy environment.

What can we do when this happens? Keep well hydrated; perhaps postpone major decisions; ask an astrologer for some insight; take Shell Essences, which are vibrational essences that understand and rebalance planetary energies within the individual. Remember change is normal, and nothing is permanent.

When we learn to remain balanced within our changing environment, and can better understand how we may be impacted by events beyond our control, then we can adjust our lives to the changing energy frequencies. Perhaps we may even learn to use magnetic planetary energies to our advantage, as our distant ancestors may have done.

Just as there are still lessons waiting for us to learn within our natural environment, there is also much wisdom to be learnt from our universal planetary environment.

"Lift up your eyes beyond the hills, from whence comes much help."

Attracting and Collecting Negativity

One unexpected problem that confronts us all, is taking onboard the negative energies of others. This is an unconscious habit, completely unintentional, but very prevalent among sensitive, empathetic people who are in close emotional contact with others.

Spirit suggests that up to 40% of the anger, fear, and pain we feel has its roots within another, and therefore can't be healed by the person who has taken on the imbalance.

We are energy beings, and *like attracts like*. So for example, if we have a small amount of fear and are in empathetic contact with someone who has a lot of fear, their fear is attracted to us, and a download occurs. We can't heal this fear because we don't have the cause; all we can do is clear it from our energy. We must use awareness, intent and also natural therapies. (The vibrational Shell Essence "Just Me Plus" was created to remove these imbalances).

Many years ago one of my sons taught me the importance of not holding the negative energies of others. He was a teenager who had just received his driving license, and had to drive to a school concert one night. Late that evening I began to feel rather sick and anxious; I knew I was connecting with my son, and thought he must be worried about driving home along the old coast road at night where rocks often fell. I held onto the anxiety, thinking that by sharing it I was helping him. When he arrived home he explained his fear – nothing to do with driving! The concert was finishing late and he realized *Macca's* was going to be shut! I learned not to take on the fears of others!

The swirling cords of energy that connect us are intended for the sharing of love, compassion, support, and joy. But because we are still carrying our own emotional burdens of fear, anxiety etc, this is often the energy we are attracting and sharing. With intent we can become aware of this problem, and use the protection of natural therapies until we have cleared all our own, often unconscious emotional imbalances.

When we feel only the energies of love and compassion within and surrounding us, these are the vibrations we will attract and share.

Now may the energy
Of higher vibrations
Surround and protect me
From negative creations.

CHAPTER 7

BENEFICIAL DIFFICULTIES

When problems arise we expect hardship and sorrow
But instead may find hope when we reach our tomorrow.
Unveiled within some problems we face
Our ideas move us forward to a better place.
So instead of expecting that life will be tough,
Remember our path can be smooth and not rough.
So look for the benefits, not for the wrongs
And your life will be full of poems and songs.

The Blessing of Sadness

When something you love appears to have disappeared and your heart seems filled with sadness, please remember it's only disappeared from your human vision. Do not close your heart to this person or experience. Perhaps they have just moved from the small range of your human vision to allow space for something greater to evolve.

See it as a step on the staircase of life you are climbing. Place your foot on that next step with heartfelt thanks for the step you are leaving behind, that allowed you to reach the next level.

When someone you love appears to have been removed from your life, know that they have just moved out of your human vision into a dimension very close to your heart, but not at present visible to your human eyes.

When one to whom you felt close has moved away, but is still living a human life, know that they have left to allow you space to grow and develop. They were also part of your staircase of life. If we choose to remain on this present step we may never know what amazing views await us as we climb higher.

There have been situations in my life that filled me with much fear and sadness. However when I was able to see the *bigger picture* and understand how much I was actually helped by those seemingly difficult situations, I was filled with gratitude towards those involved.

Always remember with feelings of love and compassion the part of your life which appears to be lost, and allow your heart to be filled with gratitude.

Nothing is ever lost in the *past* but always lives on as a stitch in the beautiful blanket of *now*.

Removing Time

As we continue our life journey we will be confronting the limitation of *time* in our 3D time-based world. It often seems as though our journeys are constantly impacted by our belief in time; it's the measuring stick for our day to day life; *How long has this taken? How much time do I have left? How is time impacting my physical body?*

As the new, higher dimensional energy is sweeping over our Planet Earth, one of the old *set-in-concrete* beliefs we will need to alter is our perspective of *time*.

Scientists may tell us that time is changing, but they may be still firmly entrenched in the concept and dimension of time, that was incorporated into our planetary energy to help us evolve with less anxiety and fear. *Time* is the *backbone* of our existence. Are you able to imagine your life journey without the concept of *time*? If *time* starts to become less discernable we may need another comfortable *backbone* to take its place; what might that be?

When we start to think about this we'll realise that *time* is the energy in which we are all immersed. There will be a stage on our life journey when *time* will lose its resonance with us. Gradually we'll start to understand that just as everything is connected and there is actually no separation, there is also no time, no before, past, or future. Everything just *is;* we don't have words or concepts for this dimension.

The less we stress about *time* we'll start to realise that it isn't locked into the clockwork of our watch or clock. The less stress we place upon *the time this will take; getting somewhere on time; catching transport on time;* we will begin to enter the flow of a different energy that is beginning to impact our human lives.

We'll notice we synchronize with people we need to meet, places we need to be. This synchronizing seems to occur outside the concept of time. When we begin to focus on where we wish to be instead of *getting there,* we find that yes, we arrive exactly as we intended, even though our watch may have said impossible.

Time is such a difficult concept to question when it has been the *cover of our book of human life* for countless centuries; the measure of *life, the universe and everything.* Each day try to focus just on *being*; train your consciousness to become immersed in *being* not in thinking. *Being* is timeless, and is the first step towards a life of complete freedom from the restriction of time.

I loosen the ties of Time
That restrict and bind.
From Time-based beliefs
I free my mind

Understanding Now

Today when you rise and open your blinds and doors, can you also open your minds and your thoughts to only reference *now?*

We receive a lot of advice telling us to live only in the *now,* but do we really understand *now?* We also hear a lot about *change,* but even positive change takes us back to a comparison with the past. Whenever we give thought to the past, this defines it and emphasizes our belief in what *was.*

So today, allow only *now.* There actually is no past or future; there is only *now,* a beautiful flow of circling energy that wraps around and through us.

When you begin to notice how often we use comparisons, you'll realise how most of our lives are lived in past or future. Even the present is only an ongoing view of the past if we continue to compare.

As Einstein said *"The distinction between the past, present and future is only a stubbornly persistent illusion."*

Everything we perceive today is our own creation and just *is*. If you don't like it, use your delete button to change it. For example if it's cold and raining, don't think *"yesterday was so nice and sunny, I wonder how long this rain will last."* Feel grateful for the rain, it's clearing all the dust and dirt, and the flowers, grass and trees are loving it.

If you think you have forgotten to do something – *"I should have made that phone call yesterday!"* no, if it is in your thoughts now, then make that call now. There is no forgetting in the *now*. Second by second we are choosing and creating our current reality. There is no *I should have done this or that*. In the *now* there is no guilt or regret because there is no past.

We are slowly beginning to realise that our ingrained belief in time and in past, present and future was developed to make our human lives more understandable, but gradually we are moving beyond the need for this outdated belief.

So just for today – because there is no yesterday or tomorrow! – create an ongoing flow of inner joy and peace. How do you feel now?

The Importance of Memory

Some memories and important, while others are not.

Often we complain *"I don't remember where I put that."* or *"I can't remember that person's name."*

However it doesn't matter whether you remember where you put something, or the current human name of someone. As Einstein once said *"Memory is deceptive because it's coloured by today's events."*

What we do need to remember is *who we are*; our individual energy signature; a composite of the many lessons learned, the many lives lived; the many journeys we have taken on this planet. No, there's no need to remember the details, they are irrelevant. Just maintain the heart-centred *feeling* of who we *really* are.

The amount of unnecessary information we are receiving in this present life is mostly unimportant. Yes, reading, writing and communication are necessary skills to remember, but when we forget irrelevant details such as where we've been; what the media reported; and our human activities; these are not important for our life's journey.

Always keep in contact with your *heart brain;* wherein lays the important memories of love, compassion, peace, togetherness, and the inner understanding of the beautiful amazing *Spiritual Being* currently walking in your human shoes. What the human eyes see, and where the human hands place something are unimportant details.

Each day please practice remembering who you *really* are; what you are *really* doing on this planet; what important messages are laying in your heart.

These initial memories are always with you, waiting to be remembered.

We do not always remember accurately because we are seeing through the emotional *lens* we are currently wearing. If that *lens* is distorted by thoughts of anger, fear or self-pity for example, then our remembrances will be coloured by these thoughts. It has been proven that two people observing the same event may describe it very differently.

So if you have memories of difficulties with another person, especially if that person is a family member or a close friend, always remember that your memory may not be *on the same page* as them. Perhaps they have a very different belief of who said, or did what to whom.

If you have difficulty forgiving someone, understand they may have quite a different perception coloured by their beliefs at that time, and the emotional baggage they may have been carrying. Perhaps your personality is now quite different from the personality you had when an incident occurred; you are now seeing through different *lenses.* That is why forgiveness is so important.

We all carry old negative childhood memories, usually of some perceived childhood event; someone important to us made a comment that was damaging to our child's ego. But did they? Or are we remembering through our 3 year old perception?

However within our hearts are *lenses* of love, and we can forgive any old negative memories we may still hold. We understand that they were received through the damaged emotional ego of that time.

How do we prevent the creation of future negative memories?

When we wake each morning we can have intent to set the dials and buttons of our inner thoughts to receive only messages of love, compassion, belief in our beautiful selves, and in the compassionate, caring world that is surrounding us.

Perhaps we could use an affirmation such as:

"Today may I journey with love in my heart,
and peace and compassion within every cell of my Being.
May I experience and share this peace and love with all other souls."

Protection

There is one important task we may all need to include in our lives, and that is *protection*. The new, higher vibrations of love, compassion, kindness, and support will need protection from the old negative, but still powerful energy of control, and rigid, narrow-minded beliefs.

You will find many people still adhering to this ancient energy; they will look for ways to acknowledge it as the most appropriate behaviour to fulfill their needs. The newer, finer vibrations of love, trust, and compassion must be protected so they can grow and subtly spread; not be stamped out by those who believe a belligerent attitude is the only way to behave.

This conflict of energies is very apparent in a world view, but is also noticeable amongst children. Those who are naturally using the newer, positive vibrations will need protection from the bullying that may occur if other children are influenced by the old negative attitudes of competitiveness and aggression, espoused by some parents and teachers.

Protection of the gentle, kinder qualities is so important to allow these energies to grow and widen their sphere of influence, until the old negative vibrations begin to lose their control.

Teach your children to turn away from the bullying attitudes of some. Search for other children who believe in kindness and consideration. The more these positive attitudes are quietly sent, the further this new energy will spread. However initially it will need to be nurtured and protected. No matter how much we might wish to defend our views and attempt to convince the negative people how much happier and more successful they would become if they followed our beliefs, please just smile and walk away.

When attitudes of compassion, kindness and trust are ridiculed and there is pressure to revert back to the old aggression, force and competitiveness. Do not fight back; this will only make it easier for the negative to attach. Remember like attracts like; smile, send thoughts of forgiveness and compassion and walk away. The only way to change the attraction towards the negative is to portray the positive through our every action. The new energy is then spread gently, quietly, but profoundly.

Within the higher vibrations
Of love, trust and faith,
In the Oneness of all, I am always safe.
Untainted by fear from the negative mind
I am part of a compassionate humankind.

CHAPTER 8

COUNTING OUR BLESSINGS

Whenever you feel a little bit lost
And your world seems somehow disjointed,
That's when you must pause and search within;
You'll never be disappointed.
Although the fabric of your human self
Seems somewhat worn and frayed,
Look within at the beauty and peace
That this covering just overlays.
When you wade through the river of discontent
Realise that just ahead, help has been sent.
Hands are outstretched, hearts full of love,
Compassion and peace reach down from above.
Your spiritual friends may be also disguised,
But doubt no more; look into their eyes.
You are each formed from the beauty of Spirit;
Know this is true, and everyday live it.

Although we may face many obstacles on our life journey, there will also be many blessings scattered along our path. If we look for them, the number of blessings will certainly be greater than the number of obstacles, and of course have more value. However the value of these blessings comes only from the value we place upon them.

If we deny them —*"Oh, that can't be right, I'm sure it will prove to be negative,"* then a valuable blessing might fade and disappear. However it can't actually disappear; it will just wait in the background until we're able to recognize it.

How many blessings have been scattered along your path which still lay waiting for recognition? Please set your *buttons* to *recognition*; *acceptance*; and *gratitude for blessings,* and your life path will begin to glow.

When I toss little balls of meat to the meat-eating birds in my garden, the magpies, butcherbirds, and currawongs catch them almost as soon as they leave my hand. But the kookaburras often miss, then stare at the balls of fallen meat. They choose to eat directly from my hand. They don't seem to believe in catching something tossed to them – perhaps they don't trust it? Unfortunately for the kookaburras the neglected blessing doesn't lay there waiting for them; I have two little dogs!

Blessings may initially seem disguised as obstacles, but with intent and awareness they will take on their true nature. How many blessings have you ignored and not seen their real value? Take a closer look.

The Gifts of Unexpected Difficulties

We may not know what undiscovered gifts await us until faced with some previously unknown difficulty. When confronted with a *sink or swim* we could discover gifts and qualities that we never guessed were hiding within. Perhaps this is one reason why unexpected difficulties arise, sometimes just when we thought *"everything is going so well!"*

By confronting these problems we might not *sink* as we may have initially feared, but *rise to the surface,* and once these problems are confronted, unexpected gifts may arrive.

Perhaps we meet someone who is able to give the assistance we seek; our life turns a corner, and becomes richer than we could have imagined.

Perhaps we have an awareness *"Oh my God that is the problem which my parents had and accepted as normal! I have been programmed to expect and accept this! No, it's not normal for me; I can change these old negative attitudes."*

Maybe problems arise and conflicts develop within family or work relationships. Again, we can criticize, deny, or perhaps take the blame. However another thought could arrive; *"this is a problem I can solve with understanding and compassion. There is no need for a conflict of interests."* We might then discover that instead of accepting conflicts and taking sides, we have the ability to see things differently and find paths of communication and cooperation.

Personal problems that arise to confront us are usually of great value if we look for the gifts they can offer when seen with the intent of learning, cooperation, and harmony. Some may have their roots in previous, more difficult times, or perhaps unresolved childhood issues. Seeing the *bigger picture* is possible and also necessary, and can create a harmonious outcome that once seemed impossible.

So when problems arise, sometimes *out of the blue* remember they may be gifts.

Continue playing your *game of life,* and congratulate yourself each time you confront and solve another problem. Continue to gather and spread the gifts of wisdom and harmony you are creating. Remember we are all connected in this wonderful web of life. Let the problems and difficulties we solve spread their healing wisdom to all.

Stepping Forward with Intent and Awareness

As I keep emphasizing, this current life journey is probably very different from any we have experienced. The basic energy of our previous lives could only be used to create very basic experiences, but on this journey we are accessing and creating higher vibrational energy, therefore greater awareness is possible, predicted, and expected.

Our unconscious thoughts are often filled with memories from other lifetimes on this planet. However we may now receive thoughts and feelings that are quite different to these previous experiences; they have a warm resonance of remembrance. It's important to notice and acknowledge this resonance. It's as if we are travelling back to *home*, a place of love and harmony.

However we are not just travelling towards this place of beauty and peace; we are uncovering, or recreating it, step by step. With every act of friendship, every thought of trust, faith, and inner happiness, each step of positivity takes us closer to our real home. Every act of distrust and fear makes us retreat back to the past.

Please become aware of each step; if negativity enters your thoughts, pause. Do not take that next step until you have corrected your thoughts and replaced them with positive ones of peace, faith and happiness; then you can move forward again.

The further you travel through life, the easier this will become, however you will need to remain alert and aware of your thoughts. Old habits do not die easily, but with awareness and intent they can be replaced.

Our life journey may sometimes seem monotonous and the same, day after day, but it's actually filled with blessings if we are open to seeing them. So when life seems uninspiring, remember that what you are seeing comes through your own filter, and can be distorted if your mind is closed to blessings and happiness.

The openness of our mind is determined by our emotional state. If this is sad and depressed, then that is what we will see and experience. If our intent is for joy, happiness, and peace, then this is what we will find. These blessings surround us, but it must be our intent to see them.

Upsetting the Building Blocks

Never forget that difficult times are often the precursor of good times. When your life seems difficult it probably means you can't see what might be coming over the horizon; the expectations with which you created your life have been overturned, changed, and now you don't know what to expect.

This is an important stage, and is sometimes the only way positive change and a new direction can be created. When we were programmed to expect more of the same, this is what we continued to create. Now it's time to move forward.

To quote Einstein again *"You can't solve your problems with the same thinking that created them."*

"In the middle of difficulty lies opportunity".

This is the reason it may appear that our lives have been *turned upside down,* and we no longer know what to expect. Will warfare continue to be the expected outcome of dissent? Is the weather on our planet going to follow the same pattern we have always known? Are our political systems going to provide the same expectations of *the rich must prosper and the poor must suffer?* Will we continue to accept the bullying that we may believe is inherent in our work place?

Yes, the current turmoil is very uncomfortable but it is forcing us to make decisions based on *"what do I really want?"* rather than *"what do I expect the outcome to be?"*

As we begin to realise we have much more personal power than we previously believed, we will begin to make positive changes. Small though these might initially seem they will spread and continue to gather strength.

Because everything on our planet is interconnected, the *wind of change* sways not just a small area, but brings the blessings of positive change to all.

Do you understand why the balance of your life may need to be upset? When your building blocks have been dismantled and scattered you now have the chance to build something new and different.

When you need support, ask for help and you will find it. There are many great thinkers and philosophers writing at present who understand the changes and have been given guidance to help us. When you need more signposts to follow, look for synchronicities to guide you.

For a few days I stopped writing because I believed I couldn't find anything new to write. Then as I walked my dogs in the park one morning I passed a lady I had never seen before who paused, looked at me and said *"you need to talk to Jesus."* I was amazed and replied *"but I do."* *"No"* she said firmly, pointing at me *"you need to talk to Jesus,"* and then she walked on.

My last book was dictated by *Jesus!* As a result I picked up my pen and continued to write.

The Importance of Gratitude

As you continue your journey always remember the importance of gratitude. It's so easy to overlook the many small blessings scattered along your path. Gratitude for these small blessings will contribute to your peace of mind and inner happiness.

Whenever you notice a blessing – whether it is a phone call from a friend or a smile from a stranger, please place it within your heart with gratitude. When you remember blessings, their healing becomes stronger; in some way they become part of you. When noticed and appreciated they add love, and inner healing to your life, but left unnoticed they can dissolve and disappear.

When we develop the habit of acknowledging with gratitude even the smallest blessings, we will also see the importance of spreading small blessings for others to find. Understand that you are not only noticing beauty and love, but also creating beauty and love for those who are following you.

Now you are moving along your life path with a little more awareness, and this awareness will grow each day as new spiritual growth is presented.

There will be many days of growth, and also many days of apparent slow, stagnant energy. This is all to be expected, so don't lose faith when you cannot see what is awaiting you around the next bend.

Each time we continue to follow our heart we will find that it leads us to a path of *Light*. Even when it may seem that life is presenting us with great difficulties, if we follow our heart, our *Inner Guide* will always lead us to the *Light*.

Whether you notice blessings and hold them in your awareness with gratitude is always your choice. When you distribute them for others, it is their choice whether they will notice and accept them. However as you scatter and spread blessings, you are creating a life path with more love, beauty and harmony just because you are travelling it. The path then becomes easier for all.

Finding Paths of Harmony

It might seem a difficult time for many at present. When life rolled along and we always knew what to possibly expect, our attention and concentration were focused on work, relationships, abundance, health etc, so even when things seemed difficult, it was a comfortable, familiar difficulty.

However, now the planetary energy is changing. The comfort of familiarity is disappearing. This really is the *turning of the tide,* and many are trying to focus on remembered things of the past – wars, perhaps illness, and familiar difficulties such as the displacement of people from their homes, homelands and cultures. The current displacement, upheaval and loss of familiarity is impacting humanity and creating a feeling of impending disaster for many. If enough people take this concept as a possible reality, they may try to create it.

During these times of change it is so important to concentrate on positive issues; there are many of these if our minds are open to them. Why do we focus on countries experiencing difficulties instead of countries that are coping with change, whose citizens are happy and content with their lives?

Doesn't it seem strange we only hear about negative world events? Why should our minds be filled with disaster, rather than good news of countries that are trying to create harmony? When we allow ourselves to be dominated by fear, then this is what we will continue to create.

We know we must notice the small acts of kindness that always surround us. Now we need to search for and study the larger positive actions, where groups of people are attempting to create harmony and wellbeing. If our media would find those areas of success, wouldn't this be more useful?

As the *tide turns* you will see that life lessons can be learned not only by making mistakes, but by finding a path of harmony and following that path. Learning by mistakes was the accepted way of the past. Many have now understood that this is not the only way to learn; we can also choose to create positive actions and harmonious changes, and then find that this is what we have been seeking.

Search for, and align with groups who are creating peace and abundance, rather than war and misery.

Acknowledging Triumphs

Sometimes we may think there is nothing new to learn from our life journey – surely we have discovered all the possibilities and hazards? But there will always be something new, different and unexpected. How could we continue to grow were this not possible? No matter how many times we have faced difficulties and triumphs, there will always be more.

Have you realized that triumphs are often more difficult for us to confront than hazards? We have such a long ingrained belief in our unworthiness that we may disbelieve our triumphs and even push them away. When others congratulate you and admire something you are creating, lessons you have learned, or troubles that no longer infringe, do you immediately look for what might be still missing? Is your immediate response to their admiration *"it was nothing really; I've still got a long way to go?"*

We need to understand the importance of acknowledging our triumphs; not from the human ego illusion of *"look at me everyone!"* but from the spiritual understanding of *"if I can achieve this, how much more can I achieve that I may have believed was impossible?"* It's like climbing a mountain; you pause to admire the view, and notice with amazement how far you have climbed. You realise that the next climb is only possible because of where you are now. You may notice some climbers a little lower on the slope looking worried and full of doubt. When they see you they know that a further climb is possible, and the view will be even more magnificent.

Many of us have been so indoctrinated with the belief we are weak and not worthy of achieving or winning, we find it easy to deny our achievements. If you are aware that this has been your programming, create a positive affirmation and speak it aloud to yourself until you start to believe it.

Each triumph is a step that can raise you higher to achieving your goal of wisdom and growth. Acknowledge and accept each triumph with gratitude, then you can move on to the next one that is ready and waiting just out of sight.

One triumph I'll always remember was doing a fire-walk as part of a Stuart Wilde *Warrior's Wisdom* course many years ago. I naively believed that a few brave souls would attempt this and the rest of us would stand around and applaud – how wrong was I!

When my turn came to do the fire-walk I was terrified; as a small child I had walked across a pile of burning rubbish and burnt my feet so severely I was hospitalized. I stood with shaking knees, and a wonderful feeling of peace and faith flowed over me. I then knew beyond any shadow of doubt that I could do this, and so I did – fascinated why coals that looked so soft and glowing could feel so scratchy!

I'll never forget that empowering experience of discovering the *Being Within.*

Each accomplishment achieved on your life journey has made it easier to achieve the next. Each is a stepping stone to a further gift, lesson or task.

The Healing Power of Laughter

When you hear words of rejection, disappointment, fear and *what's the use!* from another person, how do your react? Do you attempt to change their mind and beliefs until they can see the world from your personal vision of peace and harmony? No, just leave them be – although you could change the subject and maybe make them laugh?

Remember, laughter is a powerful healing tool. Think of something you could say or do for those lonely, lost people, and create a journey together with laughter. It doesn't matter that some might think you crazy. There will be others who accept the gift of laughter, join with you and lay down their burden of worry and despondency in exchange for the light load of laughter.

It's difficult to continue seeing the world as a fearful place when we can find something to make us laugh. Notice how small children enjoy laughter, and how popular are books and TV presentations that create laughter. Yes, everyone has different triggers for laughter and what some people find funny, others may ignore. However when our intent is to trigger lighthearted laughter in another in order to remove their worries, we will always know how to proceed.

So rather than attempt to convince those doubting souls that there is still happiness and peace in the world, find the key to laughter. Remember laughter should arise from lighthearted fun, not *making fun of someone;* it's a form of togetherness. You understand the value of peace, love, harmony, and compassion; now please add laughter to these qualities. Laughter can encompass all into a flowing *oneness,* where worry, anxiety and fear cannot find a home.

Quite often when someone has rung to tell me of their emotional pain and their difficulties, by the end of the conversation we are both laughing. Initially I thought *"This person is telling me about serious problems; am I being irresponsible to move them to laughter?"* Then I read that laughter is the most healing emotion after love. It's a gift we've been given that is being rediscovered and enhanced in these times of change.

You could think of laughter as a *quality of the gods;* something absent in more basic life forms. To be able to laugh at ourselves rather than find ways to self aggrandize is an art worth practicing.

Please open that forgotten drawer and find the laughter that may have been hidden there since childhood. Use this gift to create a brighter, happier planet.

Developing Imagination

Whenever you feel overwhelmed with thoughts, with perceived difficulties, or anxiety about the actions of others, pause, and count your blessings. Instead of thoughts of anxiety, think of a list of things for which you feel grateful.

During these times of change you may feel emotionally fragile; make allowance for this. Surround yourself with the gentle energy of forgiveness and compassion. Don't enter into the negative thought-forms or actions of others. Bless them and move aside.

Imagine you are standing under a warm shower; each droplet of water is infused with love, compassion, and the inner strength of forgiveness and positive self-esteem.

Feel these droplets with which you are being showered, removing all the anxiety, distress and fear. Every cell in your body is being cleansed, and every vibration of negativity washed away. Allow yourself to stand within this shower until you feel totally cleansed; until the outer layers of the human ego issues have been washed away, and your beautiful, powerful spiritual being is now evident again. As you move through your day, remember that the dirt of negativity cannot adhere to the shine of your cleansed aura.

I realise I am speaking in pictures, but we are visually active beings with powerful imaginations, and our imaginations create our reality, so never disparage them.

Always be aware of the power of imagination; never use it to infringe others. It's a little like painting a picture; you would always use your skill to paint something that others could feel uplifted by.

Whenever you feel overwhelmed and perhaps despondent, as you try to create your lives within energy which may feel strange and unfamiliar, know that help is always available. Please trust that your life will become easier as you adjust to the positive changes beginning to envelop our planet. Use imagination to create whatever you desire for your life. Imagine from your heart and create pathways of happiness and success.

The Value of Company

As we continue our life-journey we will need company; know we will always meet others who are on the same journey. Do not presuppose how they should look or present themselves; just feel their energy and search for a resonance.

You may be requested to join with some whose journey is in a different direction, but you will instinctively know that their lessons are different to yours. So do not feel you must join them if they request your company.

There is no condemnation, there are many paths and they each offer different experiences, different lessons to be learnt, but all paths take us to the same destination.

Imagine that life journeys are like entering a university; there are many courses available. Some students might choose to study medicine, others science, or teaching. The courses are all different but each person will graduate if they continue to follow their chosen path.

The company of other travellers and the friendships created along the way will help to illumine our path. Imagine we are each carrying a candle or a torch. How much light will one candle throw compared to a group of candles?

So travelling with like-minded friends will always make our path lighter and enable us to see visions of beauty and delight we may have missed if we travelled alone.

Sometimes what seem to be delays and unnecessary detours may be because there is a fellow traveller who needs our help; or perhaps someone is arriving to help us. Each footstep we tread upon our path is creating a smoother path for everyone. The path we are following has been smoothed by many feet, and cleared by the kindness and care of previous travellers.

I feel so blessed to be working in my business Shell Essences. I'm talking to like-minded people every day who share their experiences, and my beautiful staff are *on the same page*.

I also have great memories of working as an Occupational Therapist for many years, and also as a stay-at-home mum, joining with other lovely mums to create our own babysitting club, child-minding group, and fruit and veggie co-op.

Find friendship where there is resonance; travel together with kindness, a sense of togetherness, understanding and compassion, and your life will always flow much more easily.

Giving Compliments

I would like you to pause for a moment and consider the power of compliments.

When someone truthfully, honestly, and with words from the heart compliments you regarding something you are doing, or have achieved, how do you feel?

I'm not talking about superficial compliments such as approving of an article of clothing or a hair style, but perhaps noticing how you have responded to the needs of another; acknowledging an achievement in your work life; or something of beauty you have created.

An acknowledgement from the heart can bring a warm glow into our life. It can give us courage, and if there was self-doubt it can reassure us that our creation is accepted and honoured by others.

These compliments are so important to encourage us to continue on our chosen life path, perhaps to have enough self-belief to achieve even more. An honest compliment from a fellow human-being, who is also dealing with the same difficulties of a 3D existence, is very meaningful.

It's a bit like feeling lost and suddenly seeing a familiar signpost – there is a sigh of relief; *"Oh yes, I'm not lost after all; I'm on the right track".*

We need to be aware of how much we can help another person with a sincere, heart-felt compliment.

When you observe someone else's achievement – especially a friend's, or a colleague working in a similar field of interest to yourself, it may be easy to feel competitive. Perhaps the first response might be *"I don't want them to appear as good as me;"* or *"I'm better than that!"* These are fear-based responses from childhood, from a child's need to be noticed by its parents and to receive their approval. Become aware of your childhood issues if they are preventing an honest assessment of another's achievements.

When we honestly and truthfully compliment another's achievements, we are expanding the energy of love, which spreads a feeling of the inter-connectedness instead of separation. When we compliment from the heart we are contributing to the energy of *Oneness*. There is a heart-to-heart communication that exists because both hearts are open and both become joined within the *Oneness* of love and grace.

Faith

Faith is the opposite of fear, so in order to have faith, fear must be faced and defeated. When fear is faced it will be seen for what it is – just an incorrect belief in our powerlessness. Fear is faith turned upside down!

Once fear has been faced and confronted, the problem will often become non-existent. Fear exists only in the ego mind, not in actual reality. It is born only in our imagination, and is coloured and continually enhanced by imaginary events that may seem very real to us, as this is how we have created them.

With courage we can confront those imaginary tigers. When we look into their eyes and stoop to pat them, we find ourselves patting a lovely purring pussycat. If the emotion seems too fearful, and we doubt our ability to deal with it effectively, always ask for spiritual help, as we have an entourage of spiritual helpers always happy to help when asked.

When we discover the pussycat, our faith will develop and begin to overcome other fears. *"What else am I afraid of that will turn out to be purely imaginary?"*

Faith begins to grow when watered by belief in our inherent abilities and by experiencing the dissolving of previous fears. Faith continues to blossom as we face more fears coloured by our false beliefs and our expectations of difficulty.

When we have faith in the beauty, rightness and goodness of everything, this will start to manifest for us.

To create and grow our faith, always acknowledge the power of the spoken word. Use affirmations and speak the words of faith and love rather than just think them. The spoken word has within it the power of our *Inner Being*, our life path is created with the beauty of our spoken words of love, compassion, and faith.

When we begin to develop and express our faith in the highest good of all, we will see our fears dissipate and realise they were created only by our negative ego beliefs.

I speak only words of love, faith and trust,
And with these qualities I create my life.

CHAPTER 9

SMALL ACTS OF PEACE AND KINDNESS

As we walk our life-path day by day,
We spread small treasures along the way;
Gifts of peace, love, kindness and care,
Small positive actions with which we all share
A flow of compassion to all those we meet,
And also receive from each soul that we greet.
Small and unnoticed our blessings may be –
They won't make the news, or become history!
But little by little these actions cement
A growing desire for love, peace and content.

We need to understand that our lives are of value – in fact of great value. We see widespread atrocities that may discourage us, and we might think *"how can I, one person, create any peace on this planet when so many thousands are involved in negative acts, the opposite of love and peace. There is so much suffering."*

If you could see the energy forms of love and peace, and the energy forms of aggression and fear you would see how much freer, interconnected and flowing are those of peace and love, how basic and simplistic are the energies of aggression and fear. That is why small, apparently insignificant acts of kindness and peace are so much more powerful than larger acts of negativity. This is why these small, so-called insignificant actions are transforming our planet even though it may not be immediately obvious.

Please make it part of your daily life to create small acts of peace and kindness wherever you can. Some people will be drawn to create large and very noticeable positive changes, however don't allow yourself to believe that your small actions are of little worth.

Every drop of rain is part of a great river, and without those drops the river could become a barren, dry riverbed.

Just as important, or perhaps more so, are our thoughts and feelings. To feel compassion for other fellow human beings and to send them thoughts of love is such a valuable contribution to the positive energy of our planet. These thoughts and feelings do not stay trapped within us but are dispersed into the luminous cloud of wellbeing which permeates the planet. So thoughts, feelings and physical actions are more powerful than we may understand. But above all, our *intent* is the instrument with which this beautiful melody is played.

However, the first person deserving of our compassion and kindness is ourself. We are the only *energy Being* for whom we have full responsibility to create positive change. Once we become aware of any imperfections and begin to understand, forgive, accept, and take steps to introduce change, then what we are achieving is also combined into the *Oneness* of all.

Perhaps we have arrived on this planet when our help is really needed? Perhaps we have arrived to create peace, love and kindness? Perhaps we will be involved in difficult situations and relationships because within us is an intent to overcome these difficulties? When there is intent, all our unsuspected personal power is released and that which we call *miracles* are created.

Giving and Sharing

This message is about *giving*. Although *giving* may seem easier than receiving, some people may be reluctant to *give* because of their fear of lack. This fear of lack may influence our lives to a greater extent than we realise. There may be a reluctance to give to charities – *"I don't have enough;"* or perhaps we use excuses to deny our fear – *"I won't give because that charity is probably misusing the money."* This fear of possible lack is actually permeating many parts of our planet.

However the *giving* that is so important at present is the giving of love, friendship, compassion and a warm connection with all. *Giving* is sharing; it creates togetherness and oneness rather than separation and fear. Smiling at everyone we meet or pass in the street may seem inconsequential, but it's not. It is sharing and spreading a positive energy, that lightens the person's worries and fears, and the energy may then spread to others.

Whenever you feel fear of lack, can you sense that this fear is tightening an energy shield around you? When we release this fear and acknowledge there is plenty for all, we will then feel the freedom of release. Our planet has been seeded and endowed with enough sustenance for all to survive in comfort; as long as there is sharing rather than greed. Greed arises from the fear of lack; this fear can never be resolved by collecting more money and possessions.

Sharing positivity with others; friendship, caring, or giving material goods, spreads the energy and concept of togetherness and cooperation rather than restriction and separation.

The survival of humanity will depend on sharing and giving to reconnect the broken pieces of our present cultures.

Create a habit of *giving and sharing* within your community. *Giving* breaks the bonds of fear and begins a cycle of trust and abundance. It joins, rather than separates, and every small cycle repeats itself to form larger patterns of the same.

The Choice for Personal Growth

The awareness that I'd like to share today is the awareness of personal growth.

Even though we may often feel a bit depressed and lost, we are progressing day by day much further than we understand at present. One day we will look back at *the way we were* and see the huge difference in *the way we are now.*

Instead of focusing on feelings of sadness and confusion, or health problems that we believe are not healing, become aware of how much closer to the surface is the *Inner Being* of wisdom and strength; how much more connected we are. Do not focus on what is wrong with the world; search for and find the positive changes.

Climate change is creating much attention in the world media. It's a natural cycle, also showing our human community where we may be neglecting our planet, and what can be done to correct this, live with more attention to *oneness,* and less attention to separation.

Situations in our personal human lives that appear negative, and are perhaps creating fear and anxiety, are showing where some energy is blocked, or not flowing harmoniously, so we can pay attention and correct it.

What has changed is not necessarily the difficult situation but our awareness of it, and our dedication to creating positive change. Because this has grown over time we may not realise the different ways we now face our challenges. However we need to acknowledge this growth. Too often we tend to focus mainly on what is still missing, rather than on what we thought was lost but has now been found.

When you become aware of the many positive changes in your lives, do not dismiss them because they seem small. Actually they are not. Every change in awareness and attitude is allowing the next growth. It's like the waves of the ocean – all are connected, and what may appear small ripples on the surface are part of huge waves of progression.

As our awareness continues to grow we will also understand that we are creating this positive life. Instead of fear, disappointment and separation we are choosing peace, harmony and oneness.

Creating a Positive Attitude

An attitude of positivity is needed by many of us today. We may become addicted to the drama and negativity that our media keeps feeding us, so it may take much longer to bring about the planet of peace and wisdom we have arrived here to create.

Each time we think *"Oh that is so bad; wars are never going to cease, this is how humans have always behaved"* or *"there will always be poverty and hardship – remember "the rich get rich and the poor get poorer."* These ideas of *what's the use!* are slowing the creation of positivity.

As I keep repeating, it's the small actions of care and love that are gradually changing the planet. They will continue to do so as long as we don't become enslaved by the negative attitudes of the minority whose voices often seem so loud.

Whenever you hear of a negative action, immediately change your thoughts to something positive. You might be surprised by the amount of lovely, heart-warming actions and creations you can notice once you push those thoughts of negativity out of your mind.

Remember, your mind is your palette of colour with which you are painting your world and your life. Why paint in black and grey when many beautiful colours are available?

It's so important to teach children to notice and repeat positive actions; not become immersed in the negativity of our current media. Small children are usually automatically positive; this is how their *buttons are set.* They can also become negative if they are bombarded with negative words and actions.

Teach them to see the beauty in their surroundings and to notice positivity.

It's like collecting beautiful seashells on the beach. Ask them at the end of each day what pieces of *good,* they have noticed or have created.

Give them a *positive picture book* in which they can write or draw their positive experiences.

Once we set our inner expectations towards positivity, this is what we will notice, and the negative actions and events will cease to take centre stage.

When we start to become *addicted* to positive, heart-warming stories, and the beauty of our planet, we will begin to create these.

If human life is indeed just an *illusion,* why not create an *illusion* of beauty and peace? One we want to live in and create for our children. Let's begin to rub out those black and grey drawings and re-paint them in beautiful colours.

What are the colours of positivity? If we look for them we'll find them.

Waiting for the Seeds to Sprout

When we are travelling through a part of our life where we may think nothing exciting or different is happening, this is actually a most important phase. This is when the *cake is being cooked.* The *ingredients* we have been gathering are now combined, and are transforming into something that will be valuable not just for us but for many others. Although no *timer* has been set, we don't know how long this will take, be assured that something of value is *cooking*.

There is now a period of waiting and this is what you are experiencing when you think nothing is happening and you feel bored. We can use this time of apparent inactivity to finish any unfinished tasks. Some will see it as time to clear out *old stuff* either material or emotional. It's a time of reflection, clearing a space for something new. Others who might be impacted by this must also be ready.

All of us who have travelled that well-worn path understand there will be days when disappointment and lack of self-belief cloud our minds and obscure our vision. Please remember there is no hurry and these are the times we need to rest and restore our faith.

Do not fight this tiredness and discomfort and think you must press on regardless. No; rest and restore your energy. Only when you feel rested and restored should you continue your journey. When you become tired and weary of *doing* just sit and practice *being*.

Remove the negative thoughts which are beginning to cloud your mind, as within that open space there can now be planted thoughts of courage and inspiration.

Every life path needs times of rest, and it's so important to understand and acknowledge this need. Rest will provide added vitality and value to our lives and a chance to assimilate the wisdom already gained.

When we remove the concept of *time* from our minds, we will understand that we're not wasting time during these important intervals. Every section of our life is important for the *whole* to be created with appropriate love and grace. Resting and contemplation are just as important as activity and obvious growth.

When you plant a seed and it's hidden beneath the earth, do you think *"well, that was a waste of my time; nothing is happening!"* But of course the seed is growing, and when the conditions are right it will sprout, flourish, and bear fruit.

When our intent is to create peace, love, and compassion, these are the seeds we have planted. Our intent is much more powerful than we may realise. While it might appear that nothing is happening, our intent is taking root. Our *spiritual gardeners* make sure it receives the energy-food it needs – as long as we don't turn our backs and walk away with the belief that it's all a waste of time!

Remember, this is actually when everything is happening, even though it has yet to come into our conscious awareness.

Many of us are planting seeds of peace, love and oneness; these seeds are growing, and when conditions are right, they will sprout into a wonderful harvest.

Unexpected Surprises

As we continue our life journey there will be unexpected surprises along the way; some amazing, happy surprises, some sad and perhaps fearful.

Remember we may never have ventured so far in a human life on this planet. We are creating our spiritual journey day by day, not just following previous paths.

When you receive a welcome surprise, please congratulate yourself and give grateful thanks. Don't follow that old well worn path of *"it can't be true, I bet it will just disappear again!"* There is no surer way of dismissing the wonderful surprise and returning back to negativity. Each welcomed, positive feeling or action is the forerunner of many more – as long as they know they are welcome and expected.

However when a negative, or sad feeling or action envelops us, we can use positive affirmations to dismiss it. Perhaps it has come from an old note written in the past which is still held in our *book of memories*. Decide to shred it, tell it that the energy it holds is no longer conducive with the present energy construction we are creating.

The worst thing we can do is to say *"Oh yes, I thought this would happen, it always does!"* Then we are once again retreating to the way things were.

My two little poodles are great examples of different responses to expectation.

They are both rescue dogs with difficult backgrounds. I walk with them each day and if we meet a larger dog the initial response of Buddy, the black poodle, is hesitation and fear. He backs away and won't approach the other dog until I kneel and pat it; then Buddy trusts and the sniffing regime begins.

My small black and white poodle Panda, greets each dog and each person with joy and happy anticipation, and always receives the warm welcome he expects.

Buddy expects and receives hesitation and a little distrust; Panda expects and receives joy and love. They are wonderful examples of *as you give, so shall you receive.*

You have decided to create a life of closeness with your Spiritual Creator, to join with the *Oneness* of positive, harmonious energy, otherwise you would not be reading this book. Yes, there will be unexpected gifts of joy and also of sadness and fear, yet you will always know how to cope with them.

If self-doubt arises ask for Spiritual help and use positive affirmations to confirm your belief in the wonderful Spiritual Being you are uncovering.

Connected to the love within
Gifts lay waiting – enter in,
Trust; believe; receive and grow
Take what you need
From your endless flow.

CHAPTER 10

◆

THE HEALING ENERGY OF NATURE

Our life unfolds easily, seam by seam
Like the gentle flow of a sacred stream
The clouds bestow their blessing of rain
Then the sun warms the fertile soil again.
All of nature listens to the song of the birds
And the cattle gather in the comfort of herds.
Then once again the softness of night
Slowly and silently darkens the sky
Providing the rest on which we rely.
Until dawn once more draws our curtains aside
And we rise again to the call of the tides
Within the sacred flow of night and day,
We create our blessings, be they work or play
Our lives continue with nature's soft chant,
Teaching us gently our blessings to count.

*N*ature is the background energy of Planet Earth. All has been created, and continues to be created with adherence to this pattern.

When a new planet is created that is designed to be comfortable for life as we know it, then the same pattern is adhered to.

Everything may not appear physically identical with the *nature* of Planet Earth, but the same pattern – a series of fractals – is the basic design. This allows for growth and change, but always within the same pattern, the pattern of love.

You might consider *nature* to be the language of Planet Earth; everything is written in the language of *nature*. Those who take time and effort to understand this language will also understand themselves. To live successfully on this planet we need to learn the language of *nature;* the language that connects, teaches, and also heals.

When we turn our back on *nature* we lose connection with ourselves and our inner wisdom and knowledge.

The Language of Nature

We live on a beautiful, blue, evolving planet that is changing, but not just due to our lack of care for it. Technology has replaced the wisdom of *nature* for many of us, but *nature* has always been part of the creative energy of Planet Earth. *Nature* has more wisdom to teach than we are currently learning. Much of the indigenous wisdom has been forgotten when its value was disregarded as our love and dedication to current science began.

The healing energy of *nature* is mentioned many times in these writings. Our planet was seeded with *nature* to provide both lessons and wisdom; doors we could open to discover so much more about ourselves, and what is available for us.

Einstein said *"Look deep into nature, and then you will understand everything better."*

We cannot remove *nature* from our planet no matter how hard we try; it will always re-grow to the pattern that was set as our planet was made ready for human life.

Nature exists in a different time frame to that in which humans currently believe; it exists in the *now,* a pattern it will always follow. Perhaps you believe that parts of the natural world will become extinct as we destroy them? No, their intrinsic energy pattern cannot be destroyed and will continue to live, but perhaps in a different physical form.

Our planet has been designed to evolve, not to die, and this is a lesson also for humanity. Many of the lessons of *nature* were learned by the indigenous humans who lived very closely with *nature,* thus were able to observe its wisdom. Today we look to the science of technology to explain our lives, our health and our growth. Do not close your minds to the learning embedded in the natural world that was designed for us to discover, learn and grow.

Consider *nature* a book which has been written in a language we are able to read, because that same energy language has been taught to humanity. The lessons of *nature* can be learned through experience, observation, but most importantly of all, through allowing the energy of *nature* to permeate our inner understanding.

My personal spiritual understanding came from observing nature. As a child and teenager I was taught only the protestant religion of my parents, but as an adult I converted to Judaism as my husband was Jewish. When I discovered that Jewish customs didn't sit comfortably with me, I decided to walk in the bush each day and form my own beliefs. I learned how everything was connected, each supported the *whole*; nothing disappeared but just changed. I had read no spiritual literature at that time, but when I did I was amazed to find that the understanding of *life, the universe and everything* I had learned from nature, were well known spiritual beliefs.

Everything we need to know in order to continue evolving and growing spiritually, emotionally and physically has been written in the language of *nature*, just waiting for us to be able to read it.

Einstein said: *"We still do not know one thousandth of one percent of what nature has revealed to us."*

Sunshine or Rain?

Whether there is sunshine or rain, both are of equal value and importance. Nature controls its sustenance that requires both sunshine and rain.

We also have control over our choices. This is where things can become a little unsteady, as our human ego self is often driven by fear and low expectations. Even though we know *as I expect so I will receive* it's often very difficult for us to develop positive expectations. There's always that *yes, the sun will shine; ….but what if it rains?*

The best advice is to trust our *Inner Self*; that connection to *Oneness*. If we listen to its silent voice within our heart – (not just within our brain) we will always avoid trouble, or find the best path around a problem.

If you look back over your life you'll probably see that what you thought at the time were troubles and difficulties, in hindsight proved to play a valuable role in your present life. If you are in the middle of something troublesome, you may not see the big completed picture.

When the deciduous trees lose their leaves, is that a disaster? No, the leaves fall to the ground, decay and form the sustenance the tree needs to grow and create new leaves and flowers.

Certainly take control of the steering wheel of your life, but allow the *inner driver* to direct you. Listen, and follow its directions. Remember your *Inner Self* sees the whole picture; it's part of the *Oneness* of all.

So when you're hoping for sunshine and it rains, know that the rain must be necessary. Sometimes troubles can direct you onto a different life-path, one you would not have thought to take if everything had continued smoothly. This new life-path may bring more colour into your life, and allow you to develop gifts you didn't realise you had.

Inside every supposedly negative event may be hidden a blessing. Expect it, search for it and you will find it. Know that we are each a vital part of the *Oneness* of all; within nature nothing is wasted or inconsequential. Within the tapestry of humanity each stitch is important, and is contributing to the beautiful, ongoing creation.

Learning from Nature

Nature is so much more important than we may realise. It is the energy vibration with which our planet has been seeded, and it's our library of information. If we continue to destroy it we are destroying not just our natural surroundings but we are destroying our library.

Previous cultures understood the importance of this asset and continued to study and learn from it. There will come a time when the value of nature is again understood; hopefully there will be some left to teach us its wisdom during our present lifetime.

Within the natural formations of our planet, and life-forms that have learned to utilize these, are expressions of all we currently need to gain greater wisdom, spiritual and human growth. When we move from the study of atoms, molecules and particles and search for what animates these, we will begin to understand the flows of natural invisible energies that animate all life-forms on the planet, and the universe. All of nature is created by flows of invisible energy; it is the *life* within everything.

When we learn to understand these energy flows we will also learn how to use them to enhance our lives beyond our present beliefs. As well as studying life through microscopes, we will study how nature responds to its environment; is nurtured and provided with information it needs for continual growth and replenishment.

All of nature knows it's connected; it uses this knowledge to sustain and develop its growth. When humans learn to use our intuitive wisdom, we will happily live together with all other life forms in our environment. This is not some strange idea, but an understanding some previous cultures knew and honoured, and we must now rediscover. All life is interconnected. Humanity must realise it is part of the *wholeness* of this planet, not a sergeant major that needs to control it all.

As we learn to respect all life-forms we'll join this web of beauty, wisdom and growth. We will change our current habits of *use and destroy* into *we are one, we all need each other*.

When we discover nature isn't something to be conquered but something with which to co-operate, we will have discovered the reality of *life, the universe, and everything*.

The Value of Pets

As we continue our life journey there may be periods when we feel rather alone. We crave companionship, love and affection, yet this doesn't always seem available. There may be many conversations; however they can seem rather empty and pointless if those close to us are not on the same *wave-length*.

Our friends and family may also be experiencing difficulties and not understand the need for unspoken love and affection. Our connection with our spiritual family is always present, but we may not believe we can take advantage of this. So where might we find this unconditional love and acceptance we seek? Look to the other life-forms around you, especially the animals; this planet has been seeded with everything we need to help us create harmony, love, compassion, and peace.

Pets, and for me especially cats and dogs, provide unconditional love and support when we need it most. They ask for very little in return, just basic food and care, but their qualities of unconditional love and compassion are always present. So when your heart is aching for that feeling of loving acceptance and silent understanding, there is always an animal waiting, and willing to spread a loving energy over you.

When we realise the importance of energy we can feel with our hearts, but may not understand intellectually, we can begin to understand how important the love we receive from animals is.

I remember when I was experiencing a very difficult period in a relationship and feeling heartbroken. No matter where I was, my pet dog would always search for me; rest his head on my knee and look into my eyes with such compassion, my sadness would lift.

We have always appreciated the physical work animals provided for us. I believe we should also understand and appreciate the positive, loving energy they provide if we are open to accept this.

As we develop the wisdom to understand energy patterns and look further than the physical form, we may *see* the importance of energy that is *read* by our intuition, by the feeling within our hearts. This energy is creating a planet in which all life can flow together in a beautiful pattern, creating the harmony we need in order to continue to live and flourish.

Whenever you feel unable to connect with this, look into the eyes of your animal friends and re-connect to the love, compassion and acceptance of *Oneness* which flows within them.

Within the energy of nature
All life on our planet grew,
In the timeless energy of Oneness
I create my life anew.

CHAPTER 11

·•········•········•·

THE IMPORTANCE OF
RELATIONSHIPS

The relationships we create with nature, family and friends
Are part of a flowing tapestry which grows and never ends.
As we connect with all of life,
We'll learn to care, to accept without strife.
Often our biggest lessons will be
To have care and compassion for our human family.
There may always be conflicts, disagreements and fear;
But we can learn to mend any tears which appear.
Then as we create these friendships at home
We'll spread love and peace wherever we roam.
We are joined with the universal family of Spirit
We're never apart, we're always with it.

We live on a planet populated with many other humans. Although we are all part of the *Oneness* of spiritual energy, we each have a distinct and individual energy pattern. We've lived many life times believing only in differences and separation; this has often become the background of our human existence.

We have a long history of fearing and distrusting any differences of belief or appearance. This intolerance may still be hiding in the background of our minds, making it difficult to create relationships with others who appear different. If we are obsessed with physical appearance we may always focus on skin colour, shape, language, apparel, and anything else that appears different to our own appearance. From times long past and unfortunately still today, we have formed a habit of looking for differences; something which sets us apart from others, be that from countries, communities or individuals. When we become aware of this habit we can change it by searching for a likeness – something we like, and of which we approve, be it ever so slight.

No matter what arguments or differences of opinion we are involved in, there will always be something positive if we look for it. Recognition of this small beam of positivity will begin to spread more light into a previously dark area.

Our planet has been seeded intentionally with many different human patterns. To live and survive comfortably and safely in our universe we will need to accept and respect different life forms. No matter how different we may each appear, we have all been created with the energy of love we call *God.*

Humans may be a very new species in this universe; it will take some time for us to accept the differences without fear. When we see glimpses of *Aliens* as we call other beings, our first feeling is fear because of perceived differences. The humans who have inhabited planet Earth have deliberately been created with obvious different superficial appearances in order for us all to learn to accept these. There is no *right or wrong.*

When we can all learn to look within and see the inner beauty rather than outer differences, then the walls and fences of separation we have built can start to crumble.

Parent and Child Relationships

Our first relationship is with our parents; this provides the unconscious pattern we may attempt to create for the rest of our lives. If this pattern is one of unconditional love, then we are very fortunate, but often the love may be conditional, and these conditions we attempt to fulfill.

Although we arrived on this planet with the unconditional love of Spirit, this may become cloaked with the conditional love of parents. So the love we seek all our lives is usually related not to whom we *are* but what we *do,* hence our obsession with *doing* rather than *being.* Relationships are woven around what we are offered by others, or what we can offer in return.

Our relationships with parents are our biggest lessons; these often become the blueprints for the rest of our lives, and are not easy to change. The conflicts between adult parents and adult children can be seen everywhere today, sometimes causing more heartbreak than difficult marriage relationships. The cause of this conflict is often our expectations of each other that usually fall short of what we believe we deserve.

Our parents provide the first lessons in acceptance of differences, and respect for these differences. Parents believe they can always lead their children in the *right direction,* but of course this is not always so. When we understand that the spiritual presence is equally present within adults and children we will all treat each other with more respect.

The relationships between parents, or parental figures and children are the first stitches in the blanket of life we are weaving. They provide a pattern we are trained to follow. Of course we can always unpick these early stitches at a later date and re-do them, but this isn't easy.

As our inner wisdom develops we can view our relationships with more acceptance; understanding that the lessons these provide will grow towards creating a planet of love and *Oneness.* When we see the relationships between parents and offspring as a first step towards creating harmony and peace, we realise that these early difficulties are so important for our growth. Without these differences perhaps we might never learn the quality of acceptance, the first step towards unconditional love and compassion.

Creating Satisfying Relationships

Creating satisfying relationships is of great value to us all. Unfortunately there have been many rules and regulations regarding what is permitted within relationships. If we can release these ancient beliefs, and free ourselves to experience togetherness and respect for each other's differences, then we'll begin to experience the true love and inner happiness of satisfying relationships.

When we realise that we are all part of a beautiful *Oneness*; that we all fit together like a lovely mosaic, we can understand the importance of relating harmoniously with each other. If we are creating a lovely, artistic mosaic picture, would the tiles all look identical? Would they all be the same colour? Would that create a beautiful pattern?

When we understand that it is our differences which actually create

Oneness, we will begin to value them instead of attempting to make everything appear the same. The only *sameness* that's important is the inner love and compassion with which we are all created.

If we begin to subtly resemble the appearance of family members or friends we call this a *surrogation*; someone else's energy is overprinting our own. Someone who knows us well is trying subtly and unconsciously to push us into their pattern. But if we take on their problems and negativities we can't heal them because we don't have the source of the problem. So we need to maintain our own individual energy signature.

When we relate from the heart and allow our *Inner Intuition* to guide us, there will be no fear of differences; just acceptance, respect and harmony. Satisfying relationships are not created by *sameness* but by acceptance, respect, and connection to the love within.

Relationships with our Family in Spirit

We have written about our relationships with ourselves and with Spirit, but we also have an eternal relationship with our human family members who have moved back into Spirit. This may be difficult to understand, as we have often been brought up believing in death as the end of life, or in a heaven that we can only enter if we are deserving of this.

When we are able to vision beyond our physical bodies we understand that the death of this outer casing is the only death; the *Inner Being* is eternal. There is always a connection with other *Inner Beings*, those we might call our spiritual family, who have strong, infinite energy links to our *energy being*. We are not yet ready for a complete understanding of this concept, but if we realise that love is eternal; love is the energy, or *fabric* with which we are all created, we can understand that this energy is indestructible.

Our physical bodies have been designed to last as long as there are new lessons and wisdom to be created on Planet Earth – much longer than we currently believe. Consider these physical bodies the tools we have arrived with to build our planet of peace. There is no point in becoming fixated on the appearance of these tools; they just need to work well. When they are no longer effective for the work we have planned, we lay them aside, and return with more up-to-date tools.

But we do not work alone, ever! We are *part and parcel* of a spiritual energy and we work in co-operation with friends and family. All those working with us on Planet Earth are family members; we all carry different tools, however this community of spiritual workers clothed as human beings are always working together to create this planet of peace.

Those who have chosen not to carry these *human tools* at present are still with us, watching and helping if requested. All relationships are created from a pattern of wholeness, or togetherness.

Even when you believe that some have left the planet, your connection with them can never be broken. We are all stitches in the beautiful tapestry of humanity.

When we understand the pattern of eternal wholeness we will not continue to grieve for the apparent disappearance of human family and friends; we will instinctively know that our connection with them is unbroken. These relationships don't rely on genetics or DNA but on the eternal and infinite energy of love.

Creating Relationships with All

We now understand that relationships are actually the backbone of our human lives. We are all created from the *Oneness* of Spirit, and are attempting to find this connection that we may unconsciously believe is lost.

Imagine you have a very difficult relationship with someone who is really important to you, such as a parent or family member. It would be easy to say *"I've had enough of their negative attitude, I won't contact them again."* But if instead you don't give up; but continue to send them love and compassion; listen to their arguments or anger, show you love them regardless, perhaps one day you will break through that shield of negativity, and both discover the loving, person inside.

Then you can start rebuilding the relationship, becoming aware of what went wrong before and healing those issues. When you understand what sabotaged that relationship in the past, you can make sure that same old pattern doesn't keep showing its face again in other relationships.

Each time we seem to connect, or re-connect with someone or something, it brings a small remembrance of joy. It is often those small connections that are so important. Each little connection – a smile from a stranger, an unexpected phone call from a friend, a thank you or hug from a family member, a friendly nose-rub and lick from a passing dog, is a re-connection with *Oneness*.

We have spoken many times about the importance of small acts of kindness creating peace and harmony in the world. The reason these small acts create peace and harmony is because they build a relationship that re-connects with the *Oneness* to which we all belong. We are all part of a stream of beautiful energy; there are no words to accurately describe this, but if we search deep within ourselves in moments of peace and stillness we will sense it.

Relationships are our guide book to life; they show us reflections of ourselves; they give us the comfort and joy we continually seek. By creating relationships we restore the balance and harmony with which we and all on our planet were created.

Co-operation

One of the most important relationship qualities we need to develop today is the quality of co-operation. When there is co-operation between like-minded people amazing achievements can occur. When there is co-operation between people of different minds then the seemingly impossible can happen. Differences can be put aside to achieve something that can benefit all, then gradually the differences will fade away.

Co-operation is achieved by listening with compassion to another's beliefs that are driven by their different life-experiences, and then finding threads of similarity and strengthening these until a beautiful pattern begins to emerge. Creating this pattern becomes more important than the original differences.

Gradually a feeling of togetherness forms; we focus on the likenesses rather than the differences. Co-operation will begin to build communities of caring, like-minded people, and eventually countries will look for similarities rather than extolling differences. What initially seems so important to us may lose its significance when matched with what is of equal importance to others. Gradually the smooth, flowing energy of co-operation connects all the broken threads of dissimilarity.

This doesn't mean we must become the same as everyone else. We can still continue to create our individual life paths. If our beliefs are the higher energies of love, compassion and peace, these will not be altered by co-operation with others of dissimilar beliefs. Within each person dwells inner wisdom and love; co-operation helps these to grow and become realized and accepted. Superficial human differences can be acknowledged and accepted within the higher spirit of co-operation.

To create communities and countries that co-operate together begins with the intent of individuals. The smallest efforts of co-operation will grow and expand. Each day search for broken threads between family members, friends, workmates, and even exchanges with strangers, and find ways to re-join these broken threads.

Co-operation begins with caring, tolerance and compassion, and then our beautiful pattern of *Oneness* will begin to re-emerge.

When within the cells of my body,
And countries, families and friends
Enters the harmony of co-operation
All breaks and divisions it ends.

CHAPTER 12

REACHING THE WISDOM YEARS

When we were children and walked the seashore
We collected shells that we love and adore.
As we've walked the shores of our human life
We found pearls of wisdom, when we turned away from strife.
We've searched for this wisdom for so many years,
And often it cost us much heartache and tears.
We know we have earned it, and there's more to be found;
When we search in our hearts, what we find might astound!
Wisdom's part of our Being, and we'll never lose it,
If each day of our lives we continue to use it.
As our energy changes and frowns become smiles,
We share wisdom with others who face the same trials.

As we continue our progress through this stage of our lives, we will have met many challenges and learned to face them. We will have incorporated the understandings they offer. We then may not have to confront those particular issues again.

The energy of wisdom gained from these experiences will be planted within the grid surrounding Planet Earth, possibly making life easier for future generations. What we consider wisdom was once basic knowledge. So much that has been forgotten or forbidden, is now being retrieved. Yet all the wisdom which was once available is still there, waiting to be rekindled.

The wisdom we are accessing today is sparked by interest in what our scientists are discovering about the universe, the cosmos, space etc.

However they are only able to *see* what is already present in their minds and memories. There is so much more we can learn from Planet Earth that may eventually also be discovered on other planets, and within what we call *space*. Remember we arrived on this planet from somewhere else, didn't we? We didn't evolve from apes or other basic life forms. Those early beliefs have now been proven incorrect.

When we are ready to use new discoveries for peace not war, much is waiting to be revealed. New methods of healing will eventually be discovered when we realise that chemistry is not the backbone of healing. When doctors understand that what we call *energy,* and the laws of physics, are the basis of human creation, then they can employ far more effective forms of healing.

One day we'll probably shake our heads in disbelief at the kinds of power still being used today. However perhaps the impetus for new discoveries can't arrive until the present systems collapse, we reach that *sink or swim* point.

How can we as individuals access the *Wisdom Years*? We can begin by seeing our world with *new eyes;* not always accepting that the way things currently are, is the final creation. There are always greater inventions and ways of living. Remember we are climbing that ladder of wisdom and knowledge; each rung allows us to step onto one higher. There is a much greater height we can, and will reach.

The *Wisdom Years* are waiting just over the horizon, ready to spread their healing rays when more knowledge is requested and sought.

Ernest seeker of Spiritual truth
I hold wisdom for all of creation
To illumine the path of human free choice
When intent is for higher vibration.

Entering the Wisdom Years

As our closed doors and windows start to open, even a tiny fraction, we'll begin to understand our lives quite differently. It's as if we've been living within a closed room, and suddenly notice that there's a window. We open the shutters a little and see a very different world we didn't realise existed.

This is what's happening with many at present. We begin to notice beauty. Even though it's always been part of our environment, we've never really *seen* it before. We also begin to observe our friends and acquaintances differently, with more understanding and compassion.

We look back to our childhood; even though we might have experienced a lot of pain and fear, it's as if we are only reading a book. We still remember, but the emotional impact has dissipated. The *Being* living within our human body is starting to emerge. We are also beginning to lose the obsession with our human bodies, to lose our fear of something going wrong with them.

We have grown from childhood to teenager, then to adult, but now we are entering another phase of growth for which we have no name. Perhaps we could call it the *Wisdom Years*? These stages of life are not really defined by the passing of years, but by the attaining of wisdom and knowledge. Perhaps you know some adults who are still in their teenage years? Or even childhood? You may also know some children with seemingly more wisdom than their parents?

We now need to move into the *Wisdom Years* more rapidly than has ever happened on our planet. Although we know there is plenty of time to learn our lessons, the *Wisdom Years* are beckoning. Once we begin to experience this stage of our development, there is no turning back. When we begin to open the shutters and see the beautiful world we could be experiencing, why would we want to retreat into the darkened room filled only by our limited imagination?

Opening the shutters and observing the beauty, harmony, amazing patterns and colours of reality is the first step into the *Wisdom Years*. The next step will be finding the door and stepping outside. Please don't be upset by those who haven't yet discovered the window; who try to tell you your attitude is naïve and will put you in danger. You might wonder at their limited perception, but when you look out that window you will remember the illusion that had been your own life – perhaps for centuries.

Fortunately you will find people who are also opening the window and seeing the same vision of beauty and hope.

Continue to allow the new awareness to enter and colour your life. Welcome to the *Wisdom Years*.

Searching for Knowledge

A quest for greater knowledge is now an important aspect of our current life. We understand where we have been in this life and can look back and say *"Oh yes, I can see what that was all about, now I want to know more."*

Please understand that only by living day by day and gaining knowledge as situations confront us, will we really arrive at more wisdom and understanding. We can learn a certain amount from spiritual and scientific books, lectures and channellings. These may trigger our desire for more knowledge. However our personal growth and wisdom can really only be gained by experiencing and overcoming difficulties; by observing if the course of action we took created benefits and gains. This information is processed into wisdom, and recorded within our conscious and unconscious minds.

That which is written into our conscious mind can be easily accessed whenever we need this information during our current human life. But the information which is recorded into our unconscious, our *Akash* is recorded forever – available for other lifetimes on this planet. Whenever we face similar circumstances, the knowledge of how to overcome and gain from that situation is now already there, waiting to be accessed.

Whenever you need more knowledge, gifts, abilities or wisdom in any area of your life, just ask and use your intent to open that page of your *Book of Lives.* Those who have experienced many lifetimes on this planet have learned many lessons. That information is stored ready for use whenever it is required.

You may think *"Oh, they were more primitive times; how can they help me in my present life filled with electronic devices and types of communication unheard of before?"* What you are actually learning is to unlock your seemingly incredible and amazing abilities – amazing only within your 3D world. You are slowly but surely creating a beautiful masterpiece where every person on our planet fits perfectly into a flowing pattern of compassion, harmony and *Oneness.*

You could imagine it to be like a huge jigsaw puzzle; each piece is different, but must fit harmoniously into the whole. As each piece finds its place, this then allows others around it to also fit into the whole picture.

As we journey through our daily life, every small achievement is actually uncovering another tiny piece of our amazing *Being.* True wisdom is born and developed through each of our discoveries.

Understanding Oneness

There is something of which we are very gradually becoming aware; the concept that we are all part of *Oneness* (for want of a better word to describe this state). We believe we are all divided and separated into different parts – you, me, nature, the planet, the universe. However in absolute reality we are not separate. But this knowledge and wisdom is not something that is suddenly discovered; it's a gradual growth.

Imagine you are a bud on a beautiful flowering tree. The bud opens and discovers it is a flower and part of a cluster of flowers. Then it realizes it's part of a beautiful tree. When it dies and falls to the ground it becomes a seed which grows into another tree. Then comes the realization that the tree is part of a lush and beautiful forest. The forest is also not a separate entity but is a necessary part of the environment, weather pattern, and also the creatures living in and around it.

When we gain the understanding that we are not *separate beings* we will no longer focus on differences, a concept that causes such pain and suffering. As *separate beings* we strive to create togetherness by destroying anything we perceive to be different. This is very sad, although perhaps a necessary part of our eventual discovery of *Oneness.*

When we begin to feel a connectedness with all, we will discover a sense of personal power. As part of *everything* our energy now contributes to *Oneness.* This state we have sought to create for centuries was with us all the time, but could not be sensed through a contentious and warlike attitude. Our planet still has far to go before it reaches this realization. However when individuals begin to discover their *true reality* this wisdom will begin to spread

When, with intent, we decide to piece together the puzzle of humanity, we will feel a peaceful, harmonious sense of belonging. This wisdom will grow within us all. We can encourage it day by day as we practice noticing *likeness* rather than *difference;* also when we develop a non-judgmental, non-critical attitude.

As we search for harmony we will find it, and when we find it, know that we are creating it.

Loss, Grief and Longing for Home

Another problem facing many at present is our longing for *home;* for security, for familiarity. We attribute these feelings to a desire to return to the old, familiar, and usually negative human way of life that we have embraced for centuries.

Now the energy is changing, becoming freer and lighter. There may be a feeling of belonging to something more important than our current life; something we miss and wish to connect with again; a vague perception of that which we remember as *home.*

This is our desire to return to the fullness of spiritual energy we experience when we are not living a basic human life. Now the planetary energy is becoming more *refined* this is gently stimulating memories of our *Spiritual Being,* our *actual reality.*

You may be feeling a little grief, perhaps homesickness? You don't understand this; you look to your human life to provide answers. If you feel this sense of loss, please try to understand that it is not loss; it's actually the opposite. It is the beginning of a meld with your whole self. We are returning to that which we really are; we are searching for and finding our *whole selves.*

This *whole self* is often described as becoming *enlightened;* a realization of whom we are; the silent invisible being who has been overlooking our human life and waiting patiently to be re-discovered. You may call it your *guardian angel,* but this is another disconnection we choose to use when we are not yet ready to understand our own divine spiritual selves.

Now the time has come to *put the pieces together.* Not everyone will be ready for this awareness, but higher dimensional energies are being directed onto our planet; eventually these energies will impact us all.

Initially there may be a lot of upheaval as we feel a sense of loss, and try to correct this. There may be a return to old religious dogmas, an attempt to reinstate this ancient way of life in the hope that it will correct the feeling of loss and lack of familiarity. Many inappropriate methods will initially be used until eventually we will all allow the re-connection with Spirit.

Do not look back to the initial sense of loss, but forward to the reconnection with *Oneness*.

The Flowing Web of Love and Compassion

The information we are receiving from current scientific discoveries about the human brain is of course true and correct. However there is far more to us than our physical brain. We have a strong and unbreakable connection to the energy we call Spirit that is immutable and eternal.

This is often difficult to understand from our brain-based 3D perspective. When we connect to our *cords* from Spirit, anything can be created and corrected. This is because these *cords* or *waves* connect with all, not just the human who is reading these words. However many scientists may have to wait much longer before they are able to find these connections. They may not initially believe what they discover.

When we can relate to this flow, and understand that it connects us with our entire universe we will be able to choose our memories, and abilities. We can connect with parts of this flow to create that which we can construct for our highest good, for the greatest benefit of all.

It's far too early in our human development to really understand this energy flow. We must be able to fully access the higher dimensions of love and compassion for this fine and delicate energy construct to become available. However we can hasten that development; this is actually happening, despite the fear-based negative acts we may feel impacted by.

Imagine you are surrounded by a fine, beautifully constructed web of delicate fibers, like the most beautiful spider web you have ever seen. When you overcome your human-based negative attitudes and beliefs, you can reach out and touch a strand of this web. This is an illustration we may understand, although of course the beautiful web is not composed of physical threads.

Each time someone reaches out from their human constraints and touches a thread of this eternal universal web, there is a reverberation, or vibration which moves through the entire web. You could also picture it as a lovely, incredible stringed instrument, and touching a string creates a beautiful harmonic sound that reverberates through all.

There are currently many people in our world who are reaching beyond their 3D humanity and touching a string. Every tiny vibration is enlightening the web of love and grounding it into our reality. However it's not the flowing web of love and compassion that is changing, but our ability to connect with it.

The State of Being

So often we hear of the state of *Being*. But what is *Being*? What is meant by this term, and how, in our human existence can we experience it? When, through meditation, near-death experience, or near-death-like experience we are able to dissolve the human ego for even a few moments (which is actually timeless) we experience the bliss of *Being*. It's so difficult to explain, as an explanation puts up walls and barriers.

The state of *Being* often only appears when all else dissipates. Sometimes in desperation when we have reached the depths of despair, when our 3D life appears useless; or when we search for joy and enlightenment and meet only despondency, we ask for spiritual help and everything begins to clear.

However discovering our true *Being* doesn't need to be the result of despair and difficulty. *Being*, our *real* self, is waiting patiently within to be discovered when we can acknowledge it; when we can voluntarily release the coverings of our human ego life – those emotional states and material possessions that we believe will keep us safe and somehow make us happy.

This is certainly not easy. Start with meditation. Connect to your heart, allowing a feeling of freedom, encourage yourself to feel blessed. Next notice your breathing and allow it to feel slow and relaxed without forcing any change. Despite what you consider to be your human burdens, feel gratitude for the many positive things in your life, even if they seem small and inconsequential. Then ask your Spiritual Family to surround you. Reach out and become aware of this energy, the energy of love. Know that they are always there for you. Float within the beautiful feeling of expansion and inner peace.

Realise there is no requirement of us to *understand* this. Release any perceived need to understand or to formulate this feeling into a scientific framework. It lives within a very different vibration and must be experienced with a sense of freedom, with no resistance. We are now within a different energy where human worries dissolve. Their energy is denser and slower and cannot exist in this feeling of looseness and non-connection.

Perhaps you could picture a bird that has spent its entire life confined in a small cage. When it is tossed gently into the air it discovers it has wings and can fly. What a wonderful experience of freedom!

You can remain in this state of freedom and peace as long as you wish. When you return to your human everyday life, there will remain a loose veil of peacefulness, your worries and concerns will no longer take centre stage.

You will not need to search for this freedom of *Being* again. Just connect to your heart; breathe, and allow the feeling to float through and around you whenever you feel overwhelmed by human issues. The state of *Being* is our true spiritual inheritance.

New Inventions

We are travelling through a very different landscape that has never been travelled before on our planet, even though it may seem rather familiar to some who have travelled this way in other realms. It is important that as *Beings of Light* we remember only to create discoveries which align with the *Light* we are carrying.

When something begins to evolve within your thoughts and intuition, ask your heart whether it is of positive energy, or an old negative memory. Your heart will always direct you towards discoveries of positive benefit.

Many new seeds are being planted within the vibration of our planet by those who have gone before, who see a bigger picture. These seeds are waiting to sprout, but have needed the right climate. The previous climate of fear and rigidity is beginning to change.

A different energy is spreading gradually around our planet, one of wisdom and compassion; new inventions are waiting to be discovered. These inventions do not necessarily relate just to the physical. There are many new energy frequencies we can use to allow healing, growth of wisdom, different communication with others. These can develop automatically as the vibrational frequency of the planet becomes more refined.

These frequencies of energy surround and permeate us with a greater connection to love, compassion, trust and faith. We always have a choice of course, and some will prefer to cover themselves with the old, more rigid pattern of fear and competition. However those who choose to immerse themselves within the different, finer energies will be the inventers and creators of the future.

Do not become closed to new ideas, but allow them to evolve even when you can't initially see what may be growing from those seeds that have been planted.

Creating Health, Wealth and Happiness

Something very important to notice is the manner in which humanity is creating *health, wealth and happiness*. The creation of these important qualities will not happen until everyone realizes these are interconnected qualities, not gifts that are available to some, but not to others.

When these gifts start to be shared among all people, and all life on our planet, then *health, wealth and happiness* will be part of our everyday lives. But when some people, communities or nationalities are blocked from these resources, then everyone will become blocked in some way. For example, those with wealth will not automatically also have health and happiness.

However, little by little this gentle flow of *health, wealth, and happiness* is occurring despite the information we are receiving from our media.

Start to share these qualities within small groups such as families, friends, neighbours and communities. This will then encourage the energies to spread through larger areas. Word of mouth is the most important method to spread good information. It is then given and received heart-to-heart, and not as likely to be influenced by incorrect assumptions.

Encourage your media to report heart-centred stories by acknowledging these reports, so those involved in creating the stories will eventually realise this is what their audience wants.

Report good deeds and acts of kindness within your group of friends and relatives, and watch this information spread. Most people enjoy hearing stories of compassion and kindness. In this way we are planting seeds which will eventually grow into forests, but without those small seeds there can be no trees or forests.

Can you see how vitally important it is to plant seeds of kindness and compassion? You may never see the *forest* in this lifetime, but know that when the *forest* grows, some of those trees were planted by you.

When our Inner Light begins to glow
Then all humanity shall know
With Love, Balance and Self-worth
We'll start to create Peace on Earth.

CHAPTER 13

ENTERING HIGHER DIMENSIONS

Our journey of self-discovery has no beginning, and never ends.
We have followed it forever through its many twists and bends.
When some lessons have been learnt and we close that last door,
Another door will open, more inviting than before.
We'll notice how much more there is for us to now discover;
Each time we climb one rung, we'll look up and see another.
And when we are surrounded by those lovely high dimensions
Our awareness will open to amazing new inventions.
And no longer can negative thoughts and actions intrude
We feel nothing but compassion for each negative mood.
When we are surrounded by forgiveness and love
We know we are creating "as below, so above"
As each new sun rises, spreading oceans of gold
An amazing new journey begins to unfold.

You have come so far on your life journey – and it is a journey of discovery, isn't it? You realise your life is not just about surviving on Planet Earth, living day by day until you become old and leave. We are unfolding spiritually, as well as mentally; we are learning to understand life quite differently from our earlier years. We understand that the changes we are observing within ourselves are still continuing, and more and more knowledge and wisdom is unfolding.

It's a gradual process; as we gain a new awareness we need time to incorporate this into our belief system, notice how it is changing our behaviour. The new awareness sometimes seems to arrive *out of the blue*. It's not until we notice the different way we relate to a common situation that we understand the change.

Some people might like to keep a *spiritual journal*, and record the changes or growth they notice, to make sure they continue. But once the changes have occurred there has been an energy shift and it's almost impossible to return to the previous thought patterns and behaviour. You'll also notice the new energy seems to attract other similar vibrations.

However when you meet someone who is still enveloped in the previous energy, they seem to fade from your attention. It's as though you now exist in a different reality, one their negativity can't touch, although you can observe their actions with compassion.

When the butterfly has emerged from its cocoon, there is no retreating back, nor any desire to do so. A very different life has emerged, and many restrictions have been removed. Now it's time to spread your wings, take small flights to start with, and then......who knows where that next flight will take you?

Our lives on Planet Earth are being greatly enriched, perhaps far more than we can currently understand. This enrichment is happening because so many of us have asked for more – not perhaps in words or prayers, but in our actions and in our deepest wishes. So many want compassion; help to overcome daily trials and tribulations at a faster pace than has previously been possible. We desire a kinder life with less fear, less self-doubt, fewer troubles.

Yes, there will always be lessons to be learned, but it's as if we have now passed all the primary school exams and have entered high school, what we call *high vibrations*. Despite knowing we could now find life easier, it may not immediately appear so. There are many old insults and injuries we still carry from older times that must be released.

These are often removed through dreams, or when something in our present life triggers memories of these experiences. Perhaps we may be confronted with these lessons, but in a way we can understand and accept, in order to make necessary changes in our reactions and behaviour.

Whenever you are confronted by a lesson that seems too difficult – sometimes because of the attitudes of others involved in that scenario, always ask for help. Know that help will be given. There is much spiritual gratitude each time you see a difficulty and wish to resolve it. Help is always available, but first you must ask, otherwise it could infringe your own inherent wisdom and abilities.

As we clean out any old stains left from previous times, use our wisdom and intent to contribute to peace and harmony, we'll notice our life begin to change. Please be patient; do your best to accept the changes. There may be days of discomfort that could force you to step back seeking comfort from previous beliefs and energy. But when comfort is not found by reversing your potential, you will eventually return to the *new you*. This greater potential now available is what you have asked for. You are assimilating at the correct, most comfortable rate for each individual.

Meditations, affirmations, speaking our prayers and listening to the voices of nature, are methods that we already know work for us. But also ask for spiritual help. This assistance is now closer than it has ever been. See your Spiritual Family holding out their hands with love, compassion and admiration, not to strangers, but to old friends.

Allowing the Light to Shine

As the *Light* is becoming brighter on this planet, it is illuminating the previously dark areas. We can now see these areas of darkness; no longer can they be hidden and ignored.

Initially this may be a shock; we think *"oh no! What is happening?"* No, it is not just happening; it has been present for many, many long years, but we chose to ignore it. Now as the *Light* illuminates these negative actions they can no longer be hidden. We are forced to see them, acknowledge them, and make a personal decision. *These are OK; it's just the way the world works.* Or, *No, we don't want our society, our country, our community or our world to be involved in such negativity!*

The *Light* also shines within us. It illumines parts of ourselves we had hoped to keep hidden from our sight, and from the sight of others. Now we can no longer close our eyes and look the other way. Denial is no longer an easy option.

What can we do? Eventually a decision must be made. Do we wish to continue life like this, or can we change? Change is not easy, but facing these areas of negativity each day is even more difficult.

Once we have made a decision for positive change, we discover that the *Light Within* that is illuminating our areas of negativity is also able to dissolve them. The longer that *Inner Light* is permitted to shine, the fainter becomes the negativity.

Then, one day when confronted with issues that would usually stimulate a negative response, we find our fear has dissipated; peace and contentment wash across this previously difficult area.

As the *Light Within* dissolves our personal difficulties, it also changes the way we are viewing our community and our world. We no longer focus on negative actions and reactions, but on areas of love and peace.

No, it is not happening overnight; but as the *Light* within each of us grows stronger and brighter, this seems to also spread to others around us, and eventually to seemingly distant areas and even countries.

The negativity on which we used to focus is fading. It's almost as though by focusing on it we were encouraging it to grow. Now we are feeding areas with positivity, with harmony, kindness, and compassion, and these are growing as we continue to spread our *Inner Light.*

Our Journey's End?

Our life journey is never finished. Just when we think we have reached our ultimate height, guess what! It's not; we start again. The message is to keep all the information we have gained, all the lessons we have learned, and continue to grow and inspire others.

Remember, no matter how long we appear to have been travelling through many different life experiences, there are others who have travelled longer. It is from them that we may often learn more. There will also be travellers who are just starting their life journeys; the lessons learned and the goals completed by us, will make their journeys easier.

We may now understand the laws of science, chemistry and physics that used to rule our lives are probably often obsolete. New wisdom and learning has proved them somewhat incorrect. But even though we can understand different rules, laws, principles and energy flows, what are we going to do with this knowledge?

Perhaps you thought you had now reached a pinnacle of knowledge, wisdom and spiritual growth where there was nothing more to achieve?

Now you have a different awareness of the energy flows that create and govern our world. How are you going to use this energy? Perhaps to create a world of peace where all will be safe and no one will ever need to be without food again?

For a while we enjoy *floating among the clouds;* the freedom of the higher vibrations feels wonderful; we notice there are others floating with us. Surely this must be the destination which we believed was our ultimate goal?

Then we realise there is even more knowledge and awareness to be gained. We sense that Spiritual Helpers are beckoning; we can't resist. The journey of higher energies is a journey without end.

Our Destination?

When we understand that our life journey is not toward a destination, but *is* the destination, we can begin to enjoy each sign of progress. There's now no point in wondering where we are heading, and if we are travelling in the right direction. There is no right direction; there is just *this is who I am,* and the energy of *this is who I am* is both my journey and my destination.

As you follow this new wisdom, please do not attempt to use a map or guide book any longer. You are both the map and the guide book. Do not look outside yourself for direction. There is no need to ask others or seek advice. Your inner *complete* self knows your journey and *is* your journey. This is difficult to understand from the 3D perspective, it will require trust and faith and a belief in our high vibrational energy.

We have moved past, and beyond fear, negative beliefs, and expectation of difficulties. We can now begin to understand that our life journey is not from here to there, but is the discovery of our *Inner Spiritual-Energy Being.*

Instead of feeling restricted within a tight suit of protection, this suit is now loosened, and more freedom and sense of inner destination can be experienced.

Our outer life-journey may still be continuing, but we are beginning to understand it is simply an illusion.

As our energy circulates and flows in different patterns we realise that this is our true journey. The footsteps we thought we were creating, or following, were an illusion to satisfy our outer human-ego self. The

Inner-Spiritual self delights in *loosening the ties that bind* and feeling the freedom of growth and change, as our energy frees itself from the tight *clothing* that has restricted its beautiful flow and patterning.

We also know that we are still *seeing through a dim lens*. As our restrictions from past centuries begin to loosen, even more beauty and patterning will begin to form.

Step by step we are journeying within ourselves, and discovering our true and ultimate reality.

Accessing the Energy

The words you are reading all describe lessons, but they also contain *energy*. Even though we might be repeating the same words and descriptions many times during this story of your life-journey, this is to increase their *energy*. The knowledge is being deposited in the cells of your brain, in your heart, in your cellular memory and thoughts. When you're reading these words there is an *energy* connected to them; it is this *energy* that is actually helping you.

These high vibrational *energy frequencies* are being accessed by our heart, our intuition, our *Inner Being*, our soul – we have many names for this part of ourselves.

As you've continued reading, you may have noticed a warm, comfortable – even joyous feeling. This is because the *energy* of the words and concepts is touching your heart, and there will be a spontaneous *"yes!"* You might wonder why this is your reaction instead of *"Oh well, I've heard all this before; I'm not learning anything new."* But on another level, yes, you are. What you are feeling is the *energy* with which these words are written.

Every concept, every description you're reading is wrapped in a field of *energy*. If this is the vibration you're seeking, there will be a resonance. But if there's no resonance, you might put this book aside and say *"it's not speaking to me."*

Always remember there is no *right* or *wrong*. We have all been created with the *energy* of *God, of love,* with which our universe and world have been constructed. We are each evolving on our journeys of self-discovery in our own way, in our own time.

We might think of ourselves as *angels wearing blindfolds.* As we remove the blindfolds we will see beauty and grace beyond anything we've ever imagined. But the greatest beauty, love, compassion, and grace is that which abides within each one of us.

Creating Our Future

As you continue your life journey, it's not easy to give new advice. You are in charge of your lives, and we in Spirit can't tell you what is around the corner, or what abilities you might need to develop or learn. Only as you arrive at these crossroads and ask for help, can we then give it. You cannot see the *big picture* because you are still creating it. You can look back and observe your ancient history and see what you have learned from this, but you cannot look forward, turn the next page and see what history still lies ahead.

However you are creating this *history* page by page, and step by step. As you now understand, there is no past, present, or future, only *now*, and *now* contains what you call the future.

When I asked Spirit *"who is giving me this information?"* I was told *"We are you, living in the present, healing the past, to create the future you're already living in."*

We will often find that our heart, which speaks from our spiritual wisdom, is speaking louder than our mind, which speaks from our ego personality – that structure of conscious and unconscious memories from other human times.

We will probably make some mistakes as we continue with our life journey of self-discovery, but what are mistakes? They are lessons learned. How can we know we prefer light unless at some stage we have experienced some darkness?

During our time on Planet Earth we have had a chance to experience many different adventures, and have learned much from these varied experiences. We continue with our human lives, working, playing, and creating. But on an inner level the wisdom is continuing to grow, to expand, and to colour our human lives with more loving and eternal peace that we can currently describe.

As we move through our life with more ease and grace
It seems we've come from a different place;
From the Oneness of all, no beginning or end.
The body we inhabit is just a good friend;
But not who we are! Just the clothing we wear,
That connects to this planet in which we all share.
Our awareness has moved from the physical world
To seeing our life as a flag now unfurled
We're discovering ourselves from a different perspective
And know that we're part of a spiritual collective.
As we unwrap our spirit great strengths will unfold
We just need to trust and be fearless and bold

Taking the Next Steps

As soon as we create the opening of a new pathway, it seems something is beckoning us to explore further. It's not just opening a gate into a different reality; it's also choosing to take those next hesitant steps forward.

Yes, we can always step back into the known and familiar and close the door again. But once we have even a small glimpse into the new and different energy landscape, it will forever be calling us.

Eventually we can no longer deny those calls; we will open the door once more. This time the energy we are seeing won't appear very different. We realise we have been getting to know and follow it for some time. Even when we denied its presence, this energy never really disappeared. It just waited patiently in the background of our life until we were once again ready to acknowledge it and explore further.

Sometimes it may take one of those *sink or swim* situations before we find the courage to enter and commit. Perhaps you confront a physical or emotional imbalance that doesn't respond to the traditional healing to which you were accustomed; so in desperation you looked further and began to discover the powerful, amazing abilities that have always resided silently within.

It may take a few excursions into this energy before we feel comfortable to own it and commit to the change. There will always be friends, family and others whom we have respected, who do not perceive this change as something to explore further. They see it as *"this is not the way things are, you're becoming unbalanced!"* However once we have discovered the apparent miracles that are becoming part of our lives, we stop questioning and begin accepting.

When you need more confirmation, do some research and read the latest spiritual books that combine science and spirituality. Meditate, use affirmations and prayer. Once you have set your intent, the information you need will flow, often from unexpected sources. We are accustomed to seeing only the very basic, often negative energy emitted from our minds. This mind-based energy doesn't destroy the energy of love, but spreads a cloud, or mist over it.

When we have unblocked our *psychic drain* and allowed all the old accumulation of rubbish that was blocking it to be released, then a current of beautiful, fresh, inspiring energy will flow through those open channels.

The power of love isn't necessarily understood within the written words. It is a swirl of vibrational energy surrounding and interpenetrating everything we think, every action we take. This energy is not read like the words we are accustomed to reading; yet is intrinsically embedded within all. It is the energy with which all in our universe is created, and can never be destroyed. The closer we come to understanding this amazing energy, the further we will be able to expand its use and strength within our lives.

Arise and Shine; you have begun a new stage of your life journey. There is now no turning back; you have entered the place of love, compassion and miracles. You have come home.

We continue to move with ease and grace
Our days unfold at a gentle pace.
The beautiful flow that joins us all
Wraps around us like a silken shawl.
It connects us with our Spiritual Source
From which we can never be severed of course.
We continue enjoying our human existence
And release our fears with less resistance.
We take delight in our planetary home
Which supplies our needs as through life we roam.
When we reach the end of our earthly road

And return once more to our real abode
With our family and friends we bless those days
We created love and peace in so many ways
We journey with grace through our spiritual portal
Eternal, Universal, Infinite and Immortal.

ABOUT THE AUTHOR

Nancy Parker is the Creator and Director of Shell Essences. These essences are formed from vibrational energy imprints held within the calcium carbonate bodies of specific seashells and fossils. These energy imprints hold our forgotten self-healing information that they return to our cellular memory.

Nancy's first book *Messages from Shells* relates her journey with Shell Essences, as she followed a repeating dream of creating something from shells. This dream began in childhood and followed her for many years until she finally discovered what the shells had been attempting to tell her.

She has taught Shell Essence Workshops throughout Australia and overseas, and has been a speaker at many Natural Therapy Conferences.

Nancy's childhood was spent in a small community in the Victorian countryside before attending boarding school in Ballarat. She moved to Melbourne to study Occupational Therapy, a modality that had recently arrived in Australia. This was an unusual choice at that time, as country girls were expected to do teaching or nursing. She worked as an Occupational Therapist in psychiatry and community health for many years before moving to Sydney when she was employed as an international Flight Hostess with Qantas Airways during its early years.

Nancy left Qantas to marry and had two lovely sons. She now has two beautiful daughters-in-law and three wonderful grandchildren.

She discovered Natural Therapies after completing some workshops with lovely Denise Linn and started a Shiatsu practice, eventually moving on to create the Shell Essences business that is still continuing to grow and expand.

Nancy's second book *Following the Light* was channelled following an unexpected visionary experience with *Jesus* during a group meditation at a Mind, Body, and Spirit Festival in 2015. She has received wonderful testimonials explaining how *Following the Light* helped many people find their life path.

Her current book *Arise and Shine* is also a spiritual self-help book written in a similar genre to *Following the Light*. Weekly Blogs from *Arise and Shine* are available on Shell Essences Facebook and Website.

Messages from Shells and *Following the Light* are available from the Shell Essences Website:

www.shellessences.com.au

Printed in the United States
By Bookmasters